HIGHLAND LINES
LINES
POST-BEECHING

THE WEST HIGHLAND LINES

POST-BEECHING

GORDON D. WEBSTER

Cover illustrations: Front: *Richard Trevithick* growls uphill from Bridge of Orchy with the 0450 Edinburgh–Fort William. (Bob Avery); Back: A pair of ScotRail Class 156s pass along the Strath Fillan valley with the 0821 Glasgow Queen St–Oban service. (Author)

First published 2014

The History Press
The Mill, Brimscombe Port
Stroud, Gloucestershire, GL5 2QG
www.thehistorypress.co.uk

British Library Cataloguing in Publication Data.
A catalogue record for this book is available from the British Library.

ISBN 978 0 7524 9706 8

Typesetting and origination by The History Press
Printed in Great Britain

Contents

Acknowledgements

I am particularly indebted to the many people who work for the railway (and those now retired) who have given up their time to help me and provide me with information for this book. Particular thanks goes to John Yellowlees, External Relations Manager of ScotRail, who opened many doors for me with his enthusiasm and support. Another big thank you to Mr Yellowlees, as well as to the staff at ScotRail, who arranged for my cab ride to Fort William. I would also like to thank the following people, who have helped in many different ways with the production of the book. Without your help, what you see in the following pages would simply not have been possible:

Graham Atkins, John Barnes (Glenfinnan Station Museum), Doug Carmichael and the rest of the Friends of the West Highland Lines; John Baker; John Hanlon, Diane MacDonald, Joe Mansfield and Martin Wyber of ScotRail; Angus MacDonald; Florence MacLean and James Shuttleworth of West Coast Railways; Nick Meskell of Videoscene; Mick Parker and the Class 37 Locomotive Group; Michael Pearson; Malcolm Poole (Mallaig Heritage Centre); Andy Ross of GBRf; Peter Walker (West Coast Railways). A special mention too for those who kindly gave me not only information, but also the use of their superb photographs: Bob Avery; Jules Hathaway; Tom Noble; Allan Trotter of Eastbank Model Railway Club; and my father, David Webster, who allowed me complete control of his entire photographic collection. Last but not least, thanks to Chrissy McMorris and The History Press for their continued guidance.

Introduction

The West Highland railway has been the key link between a very large but remote area of north-west Scotland and the bustling city of Glasgow ever since the late-nineteenth century. The lines to Oban, Fort William and Mallaig have long been renowned for their miles upon miles of breathtaking scenery and extraordinary feats of engineering, meaning a trip up there is always one of the most sought-after railway journeys in Britain.

There are many people for whom the lines have played a big part in their lives throughout the years and who will forever remember some of the classic everyday scenes: the numerous fish trains that departed throughout the day from the busy harbour at Mallaig; heavy passenger trains of compartment coaches, with double-headed steam locomotives blasting their way up the torturous gradients; or the stop at Crianlarich Upper, where passengers would descend upon the station tea room as the two locomotives took water at the end of the platform.

By the time I started visiting the West Highlands regularly in the early 1990s, things were quite different from how they were a few decades before, during the period that most railway aficionados would acknowledge as the real glory days. Gone were the steam locomotives and their associated branch lines and paddle steamers they used to connect with. And many superb scenic views gradually became diminished by line-side vegetation. The mid 1980s saw further drastic change,s with the loss of mechanical signalling and most stations becoming unstaffed. And of course, most locomotive-hauled trains were replaced by diesel multiple units.

Yet despite these changes the West Highland lines have retained most of their charisma. For me personally, it was always down to that enchanting atmosphere they had – the tiny stations up on the hillside with their Swiss chalet-style buildings, approached via a subway under the island platform, and those long periods of silence between trains. And if you were travelling by road, there was the marvellous spectacle of seeing the train racing alongside you on the mountainside. I can recount numerous occasions of seeing one up ahead in the distance winding

its way around the base of Ben Dorain near Bridge of Orchy, then overtaking it as it changed its course around the famous Horseshoe Curve.

There are no doubt lots of other people, each with their own special memories, who have been left with a similar lasting impression of the West Highland lines. The proverbial 'magic' of the area has been well-documented in not only the railway press but the mainstream press – so much so that the Fort William–Mallaig route was voted the 'Greatest Railway Journey in the World' by readers of travel magazine *Wanderlust* for three years in a row from 2009–11. Interestingly, the magazine abolished its railway journey category for 2012 – probably knowing that it would be a no-contest once again! It was no surprise either that the line was specially chosen for filming the train scenes in the *Harry Potter* films – another accolade that has helped the West Highland railways to gain their celebrity status.

It is important to mention the main reasoning behind the exact title I have chosen for this book. For the first part, I use the name *The West Highland Lines* in its plural form, as the book deals with all three of the lines which make up the West Highland rail network today. Not only is there the main route from Glasgow–Fort William but also the Fort William–Mallaig and Crianlarich–Oban routes. The 'West Highland Line' is the traditional name given to the Glasgow–Fort William section, with the other two parts being generally known as the 'West Highland Extension' and the 'Oban line' respectively. Despite this, all three are often seen being referred to collectively as the 'West Highland Line' – which is not strictly correct! This matters little really, but it is important that people recognise the importance of all three routes in this study of the lines and their respective individual characteristics.

In terms of the second part of the title, I have used the term 'Post-Beeching', as I wanted to write a book which studies the West Highland lines in more modern times. The infamous report *The Reshaping of British Railways* was published fifty-one years ago, in 1963, by the then new chairman of British Railways (BR), Dr Richard Beeching. This resulted in the closure of around 6,000 miles of railway along the entire BR network. Targeting mostly rural secondary routes and branch lines, around 2,300 stations would be subsequently shut and the withdrawal of steam traction accelerated further. The 'Beeching Axe' – as the process became known – would eventually reach the West Highlands, just as it reached everywhere else. By the late-1960s, its effect was there for all to see, with the biggest casualty being the closure of the 'Callander & Oban' main line, which was the main artery for traffic between Oban and Glasgow. The branch lines to Killin and Ballachulish were also lost for good, along with several wayside stations in the Highlands.

This book will examine the West Highland lines in the period following the 'Beeching Cuts', from the mid-1960s right up until the present day. It has been an interesting last few decades, with plenty of changes having occurred as modernisation continues to advance steadily. While the 1970s saw the dust settle after the cutbacks of the previous decade, the 1980s brought the aforementioned rationalisation of signalling and massive changes in rolling stock; changes which would ultimately be necessary to see the West Highland lines survive into the twenty-first century. And survive they have, undoubtedly helped by the summer steam-hauled service between Fort-William and Mallaig – now in its thirty-first consecutive year.

Over and above that, it is pleasing to report that we still have a railway linking Glasgow to Oban, Fort William and Mallaig. These famous scenic routes could quite easily have fallen victim to the Beeching Axe in the same way as the Edinburgh–Carlisle 'Waverley Route'. Or indeed the old route to Oban via Callander. Certainly in the case of the former we saw a route closed simply on the basis that it was unprofitable, despite its huge importance as an Anglo-Scottish

At Tulloch on 13 August 1987, 37409 *Loch Awe* waits with the 0540 Glasgow–Fort William as an unnamed 37422 approaches on the 0830 Fort William–Glasgow. Happily, both '37/4s' are still in traffic today with DRS, with 37409 returning to the mainline in 2010 after an entire decade in store. (Jules Hathaway)

main line and a vital artery to a large part of the country. Other important cross-country main lines have fallen in a similar way, so it may be seen as something of a miracle that those in the West Highlands did not suffer a similar fate.

A train journey to the West Highlands today still brings me the same excitement that it always did. It truly is a line for all seasons, with its scenery and feats of engineering looking just as stunning on a cold winter's day as in the height of summer. Even after a heavy rainstorm the scenery is splendid, with the line-side waterfalls and streams foaming.

I do hope that this book helps to capture some of the magical atmosphere of the West Highland lines. At the same time, I want to show the routes in what is my own personal favourite era: the diesel era. I have tried my best over the following pages to give a good account of the numerous types of locomotives and trains which have plied the lines in the past few decades. At first glance, one would be forgiven for thinking that it was always just a steady diet of Class 27s, 37s and 156 DMUs (Diesel Multiple Units), but it was actually far from it. After digging for information, I was quite surprised with some of what I came across in this respect. Preserved steam has also played a big part on the lines in recent years and I have naturally made an effort to cover this in detail too.

Another real benefit from conducting my research for this book was being able to meet some of the railway personnel who have worked on the West Highland lines, past and present. I soon realised just how insignificant somebody like myself really was next to the people who have really been there, and done that! Not only did they have some fantastic stories to tell, but it was very interesting to hear some first-hand knowledge about operations on the lines allowing me to discover a lot of interesting facts I didn't know about the railway. You think you know it all ... think again!

Gordon D. Webster

1

The West Highland Lines: A Background

The railway network that exists in the West Highlands today consists of 141 miles of track and is largely the same railway that has existed from the very beginning. Yet, like most places in the United Kingdom, the network used to be even bigger. Not only was there the renowned Callander & Oban route from Crianlarich to Dunblane, but several branch lines and industrial railways to boot. All of these gradually fell victim to rationalisation – or more specifically, in many cases, to what became known as the 'Beeching Axe'.

Today, the West Highland railway network is best described in three parts. Firstly, the Glasgow–Fort William route – most commonly referred to simply as the 'West Highland Line'. Secondly, the Fort William–Mallaig route, known as the 'West Highland Extension' or 'Mallaig Extension'. And lastly, the Crianlarich–Oban route – colloquially known as the 'Oban line'. By looking at the three principal routes individually, it is clear that they all have quite different characteristics; contrasting not only geographically but in terms of infrastructure as well.

One would be forgiven for thinking that the Oban line has always existed in the form it does today – that of a route which diverges from the West Highland main line at Crianlarich. However, for its first eighty-five years of existence, the railway to Oban was part of a completely separate main line which started in the Scottish Lowlands at Dunblane Junction near Stirling. The 'Callander & Oban line', as it was known, passed beneath the Glasgow–Fort William route at Crianlarich, with a connecting spur at Crianlarich Lower Junction. Services on both routes also operated out of separate terminus stations in Glasgow. Services for Fort William/Mallaig used Glasgow Queen Street while Oban trains used Glasgow Buchanan Street.

In 1965, the line between Crianlarich Lower Junction and Dunblane was closed and the spur joining the West Highland Line was retained, resulting in the route that we have today.

The West Highland Line (Glasgow–Fort William)

The typical West Highland Line adventure begins at Glasgow Queen Street station. But it is not until Craigendoran Junction, near Helensburgh, that the actual West Highland Line starts; with trains running for the first 23 miles of the journey along the electrified North Clyde line via Dumbarton. Nowadays, of course, the majority of West Highland service trains run as a single service from Glasgow Queen Street before splitting in two at Crianlarich – one portion going to Oban and one going to Fort William and Mallaig. The Fort William/ Mallaig services have always run out of Queen Street, unlike the Oban trains, which formerly used Glasgow Buchanan Street station, before the closure of the Callander & Oban line in September 1965.

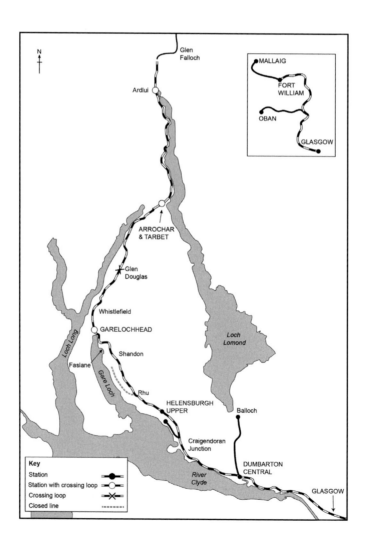

After departing from Queen Street up the 1 in 41 Cowlairs incline and emerging from Cowlairs tunnel, we pass the famous Eastfield depot, which is now used for servicing much of the ScotRail DMU fleet. Eastfield was responsible for the maintenance of the West Highland Line's locomotive fleet before it was closed in 1992 (it subsequently reopened in 2004).

Travelling through the northern and western suburbs of Glasgow, West Highland trains join the electrified North Clyde line at Westerton, where the line runs alongside the Forth & Clyde canal and the branch to Milngavie diverges. All daytime service trains on the West Highland Line now run non-stop as far as Dalmuir, with the exception of the London Euston–Fort William sleeper, which calls at Westerton in both directions. Drumchapel, Drumry and Singer follow before Dalmuir station and its triangular layout, where we join the former Glasgow, Yoker and Clydebank Railway line via Jordanhill.

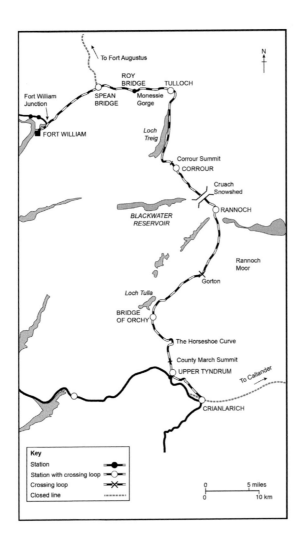

Leaving the city behind, the railway runs alongside the River Clyde estuary. At Bowling, the Forth & Clyde canal, which runs alongside the railway virtually the whole way westwards from Maryhill, enters the Clyde. After this all-too-brief countryside interlude we are back into the urban sprawl at Dumbarton. Dumbarton Central station provides another stop for West Highland services, allowing connections to Balloch – the route of which diverges from the main line at Dalreoch a quarter of a mile to the north. Dumbarton Central still retains its full canopies and buildings, incorporating three platforms. With large overgrown areas around the station which used to hold extensive sidings, it is evident that Dumbarton was once a very busy railway community.

Trains cross the River Leven on a girder bridge on the approach to Dalreoch station before the Balloch route parts company. The main road between Glasgow and Fort William – the A82 – takes a more direct route up to the Highlands past Balloch and the southern shores of Loch Lomond. Meanwhile, the main railway heads for the coast again, skirting past Cardross and the headland of Ardmore Point.

Craigendoran Junction is where the West Highland main line really begins, as we leave the electrified line to Helensburgh Central. The rationalisation of the railway is very much in evidence here nowadays, with Craigendoran station having been reduced to just one platform on the Helensburgh line only. It was once a busy station, with separate platforms serving both the West Highland and Helensburgh lines, and trains running right on to the pier to connect with Clyde steamers. The pier is now a ruin and Craigendoran is little more than a residential area on the outskirts of Helensburgh.

The first of many a steep gradient on the Glasgow–Fort William route is on the climb up the hill to Helensburgh Upper station. Although not immediately obvious, Helensburgh Upper was once an island platform with one of the 'Swiss chalet'-style station buildings that characterise the West Highland Line. It is now merely an un-staffed halt. The line continues to climb leaving the station and begins its path along the hillside, high above the Gare Loch; a landscape already vastly different to that on the electrified line to the south.

There are views of Faslane naval base on the loch, which was once connected via a short branch line which ran down the hill. Wartime traffic used to be heavy over this southernmost part of the West Highland Line, though the branch was used little after the war and closed finally in the 1980s. The site of Faslane was chosen as a naval base on account of its quiet, secluded surroundings and deep water – ideal for testing ships' compasses. Nowadays it is of course the headquarters of the United Kingdom's nuclear defence system.

Garelochhead station lies high above the village it serves at the head of the loch, and displays the typical West Highland station layout of an island platform and 'Swiss chalet' buildings. It is also the first passing place for trains on the line. A turntable was once provided at the northern end of the station, the remains of which can still be seen to this day. As trains depart northbound, climbing once again, the head of the Gare Loch disappears from view.

Only a short strip of land, past the site of the closed station at Whistlefield, separates it from another sea loch: Loch Long. Climbing along the hillside once again, the first real summit of the West Highland Line is reached at Glen Douglas, 564ft above sea level. This isolated passing loop once had its own station, with a short island platform and signal box. It is now the site of a large, high-security Ministry of Defence depot; hidden from passing trains behind large plantations of fir trees but still rail-connected.

Dropping downhill again, there are views across Loch Long of the series of mountains known as the 'Arrochar Alps'. Reaching the head of Loch Long and with the line traversing a narrow glen, we reach Arrochar & Tarbet station – often shortened to just 'Arrochar'. It is situated on the hillside at a point right between the two villages it serves – Arrochar being on the head of Loch Long, and Tarbet on the banks of Loch Lomond 2 miles to the east. Travellers will start to notice

A driver's-eye view of the West Highland main line in winter. Views of Glen Falloch Viaduct (right) and County March Summit (below). (Author, taken during a cab ride with permission of ScotRail)

a very familiar pattern with most of the stations on the line; Arrochar, like Garelochhead, has a compact layout with an island platform, reached via a subway.

Upon leaving Arrochar, the West Highland Line begins winding its way along the side of Loch Lomond, which is 23 miles long and the largest loch in Scotland. Meanwhile, Ben Lomond can be seen towering across the opposite side of the water – 3,192ft above sea level and Scotland's most southerly 'Munro' (one of a number of mountains over 3,000ft, listed by, and named after, Sir Hugh Munro). The views of such landmarks today are rather limited due to line-side vegetation, though the railway is at least a much safer bet than the adjoining A82 – which takes a decidedly treacherous course, bending sharply along the very edge of the loch as far as Ardlui.

At Inveruglas, the line crosses over four large pipes which run down the hillside, connecting to an adjoining turbine house as part of the Loch Sloy hydroelectric power scheme: the largest of its kind in the UK. It was built immediately after the Second World War and whilst not being the most aesthetically pleasing structure, makes for an impressive sight nevertheless. The railway then proceeds to cross the eight-arch Creag an Ardain Viaduct – the only arched viaduct on the whole route between Craigendoran and Fort William. The structure was reportedly built this way to minimise the railway's intrusion on the beautiful landscape alongside Loch Lomond. Its castellated parapets are especially worthy of note. The adjoining Creag an Ardain Tunnel – 47yd long – is one of only two on the route to Fort William.

Ardlui is the point at which Loch Lomond comes to an end. Its island platform is another one unfortunately bereft of its station building, though there are still remnants of the former goods yard. It serves as a base for both hillwalkers and the adjoining marina on the loch, which can be glimpsed through the trees before northbound trains begin their 15-mile ascent of Glen Falloch. Glen Falloch Viaduct carries the line high over the Dubh Eas Gorge and with its centre span towering 144ft above the ground, it reaches a height only 7ft less than that of the Forth Bridge. Remains of the ancient Caledonian Pine Forest can also be seen from the train window just before the line reaches the top of the glen.

At Crianlarich, the famous station tea room on the platform makes use of the main building, while further activity ensues when today's Sprinter trains are split and combined here – with respective portions for Oban and Fort William. The station was formerly known as Crianlarich Upper, with the other station down the hill on the Callander & Oban line known as Crianlarich Lower. The Lower closed in September 1965 and ever since then the Oban trains have taken the route of the West Highland, diverging from Crianlarich Upper on the former linking spur at the north end of the island platform. While the Oban line curves sharply to the west, the West Highland Line strikes northwards over two more viaducts, before itself taking a sharp ninety-degree curve to reach the opposite side of the Fillan valley.

Class 37 No 37404 *Ben Cruachan* tackles the final quarter of a mile towards County March Summit with the 1810 Fort William–Glasgow Queen Street, on the bright summer's evening of Saturday 4 June 1988. From Sundays through to Fridays, this 1810 departure formed the overnight sleeper service to London Euston. (David Webster)

From here, views open up to passengers of the Oban line threading its way along in the same direction as far as Tyndrum, accompanied by the River Fillan. With most of today's services joining or splitting at Crianlarich, the resultant timetabling allows for the Oban portion to often be seen making its way across the valley at the same time as the Fort William one on the opposite side. The latter line skirts the mountainside, crossing two more lofty viaducts along the way. These viaducts follow the same design as most of the others on the route: that of lattice steel trusses and built over concrete piers, in a style unique to the West Highland Railway.

Tyndrum Upper is another station on the line which has had its name altered. The introduction of radio signalling in 1988 saw its name reversed to become Upper Tyndrum, so as to avoid it becoming confused in radio messages with Tyndrum Lower station on the Oban line. It once had goods sidings located on a lower level, along with camping coaches for many years. What is still apparent today is a real lack of any civilisation in the station vicinity, as Upper Tyndrum lies high up on the hillside, a good distance from the village on the valley floor.

The Oban line now disappears into the distance behind the mountains as the West Highland route climbs at a gradient of 1 in 60 towards County March Summit, 1,024ft above sea level. These days it marks the boundary between the districts of Stirlingshire to the south and Argyll & Bute to the north, with the road, railway and the West Highland Way running close and parallel, before the railway winds its way around the famous Horseshoe Curve under the flanks of Ben Odhar and Ben Dorain. This stretch of line is best seen from the train window, with the curving track and its intervening viaducts seen up ahead in the distance before it traverses the bend, then once again from behind as the train reaches the opposite side of the glen.

It is a desolate landscape north of Tyndrum, interrupted only briefly by the hamlet of Bridge of Orchy – another hillside station and our next passing place on the line. Northbound trains face another climb out of here, with the railway continuing to cling to the hillside before the terrain flattens out over Rannoch Moor. The A82 road, and for that matter the West Highland Way, head off in a different direction, past Loch Tulla and the distant mountain range known as the Black Mount. We will not meet the A82 again until the outskirts of Fort William, as it takes a route through the mountains of Glen Coe.

The section of line over Rannoch Moor was the most difficult to build on the entire line. The ancient Caledonian pine forest used to cover the entire moor, but this was swept away, leaving only a bare expanse: 50sq. miles of heather, rivers and peat bogs. The land here was so waterlogged in fact that the navvies had to float the railway across the moor on a mattress of brushwood and tree roots, added to thousands of tons of ash and soil, the latter obtained from cuttings on the line. It is also an area rich with wildlife – grouse and red deer are often visible from the train.

There is a crossing loop on the middle of the moor at Gorton, which used to be essentially a private halt not featured in the public timetable. There was never any real community here except for a few scattered cottages occupied by railwaymen and shepherds, whose children attended a makeshift school made out

Rannoch station, with Class 156 Sprinter No 156492 calling on 8 October 2004. (Author)

In its BR guise as No 62005, the NELPG's K1 mogul performs a run-past on a private photographer's charter near Corrour Summit, October 2004. (Bob Avery)

of an ex-Great North of Scotland Railway coach body on the station platform. Being an extremely remote place with no linking road, any supplies for the locals had to be dropped off by passing engine drivers!

The line descends for a few miles after Gorton, before another uphill climb ensues on the approach to Rannoch station. Rannoch marks the end point for the B846 single-track road to Pitlochry, while a pathway on its western side leads to Loch Laidon. The well-maintained station still retains its West Highland Railway signal cabin and main building, the latter of which was formerly used on alternate Sundays for religious services, the minister travelling in from Bridge of Gaur, 6 miles away. A couple of sidings survive in regular use by the Permanent Way Department. The platform offers a good view of the railway as it heads north across Rannoch Viaduct – 584ft in length and the longest on the line.

The surrounding snow fences on the moor are an indication of just how bad the winters can be in this part of the world, especially at the Cruach Rock cutting near Rannoch. During the first few winters after the line's opening, the cutting became blocked by drifting snow on several occasions. As a result, a snow shed was placed here to protect the line and is still in situ today – the only one of its type in the UK. The track then climbs further to reach Corrour – the highest station on the entire British railway network. It is also one of the most remote, though very much a popular destination with the hillwalking fraternity, with a trail leading to the nearby Loch Ossian youth hostel and shooting lodge. The station, despite its isolation on the moor, boasts a popular restaurant and bunkhouse, though the nearest road is 17 miles away. The highest point on the line – Corrour Summit – lies immediately to the north of the station, at 1,350ft above sea level.

Now dropping down the gradient towards Loch Treig, the railway enjoys another change of scenery as Rannoch Moor is left behind. The railway takes a course along the hillside high above the loch, similar to earlier parts of the journey, before reaching the second of the two tunnels on the route at Fersit. The tunnel was actually built in 1932, due to the track being realigned over a short section here as part of the Lochaber hydroelectric power scheme, which saw Loch Treig's water level raised by over 30ft. Originally the line ran lower down on the loch side, with the old trackbed nowadays usually underwater. The hydroelectric scheme was built to provide power for the Lochaber aluminium works, which also had its own narrow gauge railway running from a terminus on the shores of the loch. It climbed for 19 miles over the mountains to Fort William, where it met another short line running to the shores of Loch Linnhe. After the smelter was built in 1929, the railway was used for maintaining the huge 15-mile-long pipeline that runs from Loch Treig to the factory. The line was eventually closed in 1977.

Tulloch station was originally named 'Inverlair' when the West Highland Line first opened in 1894. That same year, the West Highland Railway proposed to build a 32-mile branch line from here to Kingussie on the Highland Main Line from Perth to Inverness. The Highland Railway thwarted the plans, but the West Highland still had the audacity to erect nameboards at the newly renamed Tulloch station that read 'Tulloch for Kingussie'. Perhaps as a result of its hoped-for junction status, Tulloch has the standard station layout of two platforms that is more common to the Oban and Mallaig routes. It still boasts a sizeable 'Swiss chalet' station building and former signal cabin, with the former superbly preserved and in use as a bunkhouse. Typical of many rural stations, the two platforms are linked via a barrow crossing, not a footbridge.

Beyond Tulloch, the line takes a westerly direction through Glen Spean to reach Fort William, with the wooded valley and meandering river contrasting sharply to the vast wastelands of Rannoch Moor not long left behind. A most spectacular feature along this stretch of line is where the A86 road, railway and River Spean come together to squeeze through the narrow Monessie Gorge. Spectacular views open up from the train window as the railway eases along the edge of the river on a steep retaining wall, with the waterfalls gushing down below. Wild rainstorms in the past have seen the Spean flood up to rail level here.

Only 3 miles separate the final two stops on the line, the first of which is Roy Bridge – another which formerly boasted the twin-platformed layout and crossing loop but is now reduced to a single platform and bus stop-style waiting shelter. Spean Bridge retains both its platforms and crossing loop, together with an immaculate station building now used as a restaurant. It was from here that a 24-mile branch line ran northwards to Fort Augustus. Built with the most lavish infrastructure, it was the intention that this branch would eventually run all the way up the Great Glen to Inverness, linking Fort William with the Highland capital. This never happened and the line as far as Fort Augustus did not generate much at all in the way of revenue, resulting in its closure to passengers in 1933 and to freight in 1946.

As we draw towards the end of our journey, the landscape is dominated by the peak of Ben Nevis: the tallest mountain in the British Isles at 4,406ft above sea level. Another quite striking landmark is the huge aluminium smelter on the outskirts of Fort William, today operated by Rio Tinto Alcan and served by the railway on a daily basis. It was a prime target for German bombing raids during the Second World War – a fake smelter was even built at nearby Torlundy to fool the enemy into thinking they had found the real thing. One failed raid saw a German bomb dropped near Morar, with the pilot thought to have mistaken a hillside fire for the factory.

Fort William Junction (formerly named Mallaig Junction) sees the line from Mallaig join the single track for the final mile into Fort William station. The town of Fort William is the second largest settlement in the Highlands behind Inverness and takes its name from King William of Orange, who occupied the original military fort here on the shores of Loch Linnhe. Originally built in 1654, the fort was largely knocked down to make way for the railway when its construction began, with the old steam locomotive depot occupying the site. Ironically, there

Sprinters 156476/499 pass Fort William Junction signal box on 3 April 2013 with the 1605 Mallaig–Glasgow, after reversal at Fort William station. The box was refurbished in 2000, when it was repainted, with new windows and outside steps. It is the last remaining mechanical box in the West Highlands. (Author)

EARLY HISTORY

The original plan for a railway to Fort William was not to cross Rannoch Moor but to take the even more dramatic course along the side of the mountains through Glen Coe. The company at the helm of this proposal was the Glasgow & North Western Railway, who planned not only to build a railway from Glasgow to Fort William, but continue past Fort William up the Great Glen to Inverness. It would strike a course immediately northwards from Glasgow, through Milngavie, Strathblane, Drymen and up the eastern side of Loch Lomond. Thereafter it would reach Crianlarich and Tyndrum, reaching Fort William via Glen Coe and Ballachulish.

Parliament rejected the Glasgow & North Western's proposal of 1884. This was largely thanks to the Highland Railway, who had their own route from Glasgow to Inverness and shuddered at the thought of a rival line that was 47 miles shorter. But the fact was that the community of Lochaber needed a railway. The north-west Highlands was a largely undeveloped area, with poor roads and the nearest railway station to Fort William some 50 miles away at Kingussie on the Highland Railway's own line. A coach used to meet the train here each day to transport the mail and newspapers to Fort William, and it often wouldn't get back there until the evening – or in the case of bad weather, the following day!

It was not until three years later that another proposal was made for a line to Fort William. This time it was a company called the West Highland Railway, who proposed a new route leaving existing North British Railway metals at Craigendoran and striking up the west side of Loch Lomond via Arrochar. It too would head via Crianlarich and Tyndrum, but at Bridge of Orchy it would cross the peat bogs directly across Rannoch Moor then strike immediately west through Tulloch and Glen Spean before reaching Fort William. There was no intention of extending the line to Inverness this time – a factor which proved decisive and the second parliamentary Bill for the line's construction was duly passed on 12 August 1889.

are still remains of the fort today while the steam shed was swept away many years ago. These days, Fort William is the outdoor capital of the UK, being at the foot of the country's highest mountain and the end point for the West Highland Way. For many train travellers, it is journey's end on one of the world's most scenic routes. Though for many the best is yet to come, for Mallaig and the Sound of Sleat still lie some 40 miles ahead.

The West Highland Extension Line (Fort William–Mallaig)

Leaving Fort William, trains for Mallaig retrace the route back to Glasgow for one mile, until the Mallaig route diverges at Fort William Junction (formerly named Mallaig Junction). Nowadays it would seem more logical for Fort William to be a

Like the Glasgow & North Western Railway proposal of 1884, the West Highland Railway would allow operating powers over the line to the North British Railway. The engineering was appointed to Formans & McCall of Glasgow and the contracting to Lucas & Aird of London. The first sod on the new line north of Craigendoran was cut on 23 October 1889 by the Rt Hon. Lord Abinger, Chairman of the West Highland Railway company, near Fort William. His Lordship used a famous silver spade, handed to him by Mr Aird MP of the contractors.

The West Highland main line was built within the next few years over an uncompromising landscape of mountains, lochs and peat bogs. The engineers were desperate to avoid the use of bridges and tunnels as much as possible, on account of such a tight budget to adhere to. It was for this reason that the West Highland Line gained one of its most recognisable landmarks between Tyndrum and Bridge of Orchy – the Horseshoe Curve. The line had to be built on a ledge which skirted along the edge of the mountains here, crossing two viaducts and taking a virtual 180 degree turn to reach the other side of the glen. The alternative would have been one very lengthy viaduct crossing straight through the glen, but the budget ruled this out.

After construction of the line was well underway on Rannoch Moor, the West Highland Railway reached a real financial crisis. The contractors requested more money, but none was available. Fortunately one of the railway's directors, J.A. Renton, came to the rescue, donating part of his personal fortune to get the line completed. As a tribute to him, the navvies had a small monument built at the end of the platform at Rannoch station – a large rock with a sculpture of Mr Renton's head carved into it, which remains to this day.

The completed West Highland Line was finally opened to the public on 7 August 1894. The official ceremonial opening took place four days later, on 11 August, when a ten-coach train was hauled from Glasgow, arriving at a temporary platform at Fort William to the sound of cheering crowds and bagpipes.

through station rather than a terminus. Most passenger trains run today as through services all the way between Glasgow and Mallaig, requiring to be reversed on departure from Fort William – a relatively straightforward practice with today's Sprinter DMUs, but less so during the days of loco-hauled trains, where run-rounds or a second locomotive would be required. The West Highland Line was built with the intention of the route coming to an end here – it was not until a few years later that a decision was made to reach Mallaig. It is for this reason that Fort William was built as a north-facing terminus.

With the Mallaig Extension beginning in earnest at Fort William Junction, we pass the junction yard which is used for shunting freight traffic. Adjacent to this is Tom-na-Faire depot, which has for many years been the servicing point for the steam locomotives hauling summer excursions over the line. A girder viaduct carries us over the River Lochy as the railway curves towards its first

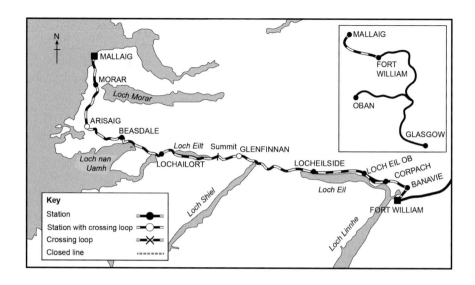

stop at Banavie. The first mile of railway on our journey so far was originally part of the short branch line to Banavie Pier, but the building of the line between here and Mallaig saw the pier branch become nothing more than a short stub. What was left of the line closed in 1939 and there is virtually no trace left of its former junction.

At the end of the platform at Banavie station is a large signal box which is the nerve centre for the Radio Electronic Token Block (RETB) signalling system, which nowadays controls train movements over all of the lines north of Craigendoran. At this point, trains cross a swing bridge over the Caledonian Canal, which runs for some 60 miles between Loch Linnhe and the Beauly Firth. There is a good view of the canal travelling up the hill adjacent to the bridge on a flight of eight locks known as 'Neptune's Staircase', while at the other end it flows into its southernmost exit at Corpach, another suburb of Fort William.

A level crossing is traversed next to the single platform of Corpach station, serving a village once dominated by a massive pulp and paper mill that provided the West Highland lines with most of their freight traffic. Leaving here, the surrounding buildings disappear and Loch Linnhe segues into Loch Eil, the railway skirting its banks for the next few miles on virtually level track. The halt at Loch Eil Outward Bound was built in the 1980s to serve the adjacent outdoor centre, actually being constructed by young volunteers from the centre. The request stop of Locheilside further down the loch is equally basic, this time with a 'bus shelter' replacing its original station building.

After reaching the end of Loch Eil, the first true climb on the Mallaig Extension ensues on the approach to Glenfinnan. Without a doubt the best-known engineering feat on the line, the 416yd-long, 21-arch Glenfinnan Viaduct

First ScotRail-liveried 156476 brings up the rear of the four-car 0903 Glasgow–Mallaig service at Loch Eil Outward Bound station on 3 April 2013. The short platform length at this tiny halt means that passengers boarding or alighting must use the doors on the rear carriage. (Author)

lies in a spectacular setting overlooking the shores of Loch Shiel. Set on a sharp 12 chain curve, it carries the railway to the other side of the glen, reaching a height 100ft above the River Finnan below. The average tourist will most likely know the viaduct for its appearances in popular culture such as the *Harry Potter* films. For historians and rail fans, however, it is most significant for being the first ever railway viaduct built in the UK using mass concrete.

It was at Glenfinnan, in 1745, that Bonnie Prince Charlie and his men raised the Jacobite standard, before his subsequent rebellion against the British throne ended at the Battle of Culloden. The tall Glenfinnan Monument stands today on the shores of Loch Shiel as a lasting tribute to the Jacobites. It was erected in 1815 and is now complete with its own visitor centre.

Following the viaduct, trains face a climb of 1 in 45 to 1 in 50 to reach Glenfinnan station. Possessing one of only two crossing loops on the line after Fort William Junction, Glenfinnan has changed remarkably little over the years. The line is still climbing through the station so any westbound trains stopping here face a restart right on the middle of this fearsome gradient.

The line continues in a westerly direction, bending round a number of sharp curves before plunging into two short tunnels. This marks the highest summit on the line, 361ft above sea level, with it thereafter dropping downhill at 1 in 50 towards the shores of Loch Eilt. This loch is characterised by its number of small islands and a short causeway which carries the railway around part of its southern shore, while the A830 road skirts the other side. The rocky outcrops in the surrounding hills are a common feature most of the way from Fort William to Mallaig, as are the number of check rails on the tight curves of the track.

Sprinters 156499/476 head west near Glenfinnan on 3 April 2013. Note the massive hillside fire in the background, following a long period of very dry weather. (Author)

No 44767 *George Stephenson* climbs at 1 in 50 past the rockface near Polnish on the 'Jacobite' to Mallaig, 10 July 1997. (Jules Hathaway)

The River Ailort, a tributary of Loch Eilt, follows the line towards Lochailort. The village here was the site of the biggest construction camp on the Mallaig Extension when the line was being built and the surrounding area was used during the Second World War as a commando training ground. The station has been vastly reduced – losing its main building, signal box, loop and Up platform – and is now a request stop.

In the next 9 miles that follow towards Arisaig, there is a total of eight tunnels, which tells us something about the nature of the terrain. On the outskirts of Lochailort, the line passes the lonely little church of Our Lady of the Braes, which stands alone on the middle of the moor. Having not been in use for many a year, this B-listed building is now in private hands. Just beyond, the railway hugs Loch Dubh – known as the Black Loch – as it heads into a heavily-wooded area away from the main road.

There are some superb views out to the Sound of Arisaig at the edge of Loch nan Uamh – Gaelic name for 'Loch of the Caves'. It was here, in 1745, that Bonnie Prince Charlie first arrived on mainland Britain, and the nearby 'Prince's Cairn' marks the spot where he departed the shores for good, being exiled to France after the Battle of Culloden. The eight-arch Loch nan Uamh (or Gleann Mama) Viaduct is another magnificent feat of engineering, built of concrete similar to that at Glenfinnan. At the viaduct's northernmost span the line plunges straight into a tunnel – the sort of scene that is quite rare on Britain's railways.

The short 1 in 48 climb up the Beasdale Bank represents one of the biggest challenges for locomotive crews on the Extension, such as on the steam-hauled 'Jacobite', especially when rail conditions are not at their best. Beasdale station lies at the head of the gradient – a request stop that used to be a private station built to serve the nearby Arisaig House. As the gradient eases, the line plunges into Borrodale Tunnel: the longest tunnel on the Extension at 349yd. Its namesake viaduct has one single arch at a huge span of 127ft, carrying the line high over the Borrodale Burn.

The second and final passing place on the line after Fort William Junction is at Arisaig: the most westerly station on the British railway network. Displaying the sort of compact layout that typifies stations on the Mallaig Extension, its two platforms are linked via a barrow crossing similar to that at Glenfinnan. Arisaig also benefited from refurbishment in recent years; its main building and Up waiting room have been immaculately preserved, while the disused signal box still stands proud at the southern end.

The line turns northerly at Arisaig before dropping downhill on to Keppoch Moss, where passengers can get their first glimpse of the Atlantic Ocean.

Both ScotRail and Network Rail have a presence at Mallaig on 7 February 2013, with 156458 having just arrived on the 0821 service from Glasgow. Whilst the original station canopy and screen wall have gone, a new booking hall and waiting shelter have been added. (Author)

The boggy terrain here posed a similar problem to the builders of the line as that further south at Rannoch Moor, with brushwood and turf used to form a trackbed. The A830 road takes a course along the opposite side of the moss before joining the railway again at Morar.

Crossing another short concrete viaduct over the River Morar, we traverse a level crossing as the train slows for the village station. Loch Morar is the deepest freshwater loch in Scotland and there are even tales of it being inhabited by a monster, similar to Loch Ness. The famous 'silver sands' around Morar Bay give way to dramatic views of the small isles Eigg and Rhum, as the line coasts downhill for the final 2 miles into Mallaig.

Mallaig's very existence is owed in no small part to the railway, which rapidly boosted the local population and economy when it arrived in 1901. The village

EARLY HISTORY

While the West Highland main line had provided a much-needed transport link between Fort William and Glasgow, the fishing trade in the north-west Highlands still had no direct and reliable means of transport to the markets in the south. To travel by boat from the fishing grounds around Mallaig and the Small Isles to Fort William was an arduous 100 mile-long trip, as the only route available was a circuitous one round by the Sound of Mull. Furthermore, the residents of the sparsely-populated land north of Fort William had to contend with a seven-hour journey from the Highland town to Arisaig by coach (which only operated three times a week), over Thomas Telford's original road of 1815. In addition to this, the West Highland Railway believed that potential fish traffic handled by the railway from a harbour north of Fort William would give the existing line to Glasgow a much-needed cash boost, as its early years had not generated an adequate return.

To the north, a new harbour would be built specifically for rail transport of the local herring catches and the site of Roshven was selected, around 30 miles from Fort William between Loch Ailort and the Sound of Arisaig. The plan to use this site was quashed by local landowners and an alternative location was selected further north at Mallaig Bay. This formed the basis for the West Highland Railway (Mallaig Extension) Act of 1894, which was accepted in parliament. However, for the line to be able to pay its way, financial support from the government was vital. The issue of subsidies caused a great deal of political squabbling and delayed the line's construction for a further two years. It was not until 14 August 1896 that the Guarantee Bill was accepted and work could finally begin.

The Tory government provided a guaranteed return for shareholders of the line and a grant of £30,000 towards the new £45,000 harbour being built at Mallaig. The industrial heartland of Glasgow provided the workforce for construction of the new railway; the contractors Robert McAlpine & Sons and engineers Simpson & Wilson both hailing from the city. They would build the line as a long extension to the existing 1¾ mile branch continues to be most well-known for its status in the fishing trade and was at one stage the busiest herring port in Europe, with the railway being the prime source of transport. Several train-loads a day were not uncommon until all of the traffic moved to road haulage in 1965. The fishing itself declined dramatically too, partly due to a ban on herring catches off the west coast of Scotland in 1978. However, prawns sourced from the nearby isles still provide welcome business in Mallaig harbour today.

The late 1980s saw the building of a new section of road into the village, with the A830 now taking a route over the rocky shoreline alongside the railway. The seaside terminus station has always had a single island platform, though it no longer retains its canopy and side wall that once provided protection from the elements at the far end. Once holding a locomotive shed and a span of sidings

line from Fort William to Banavie Pier, which was opened on 1 June 1895, almost a year after the Glasgow–Fort William route.

The first sod on the Mallaig Extension was cut by Lady Margaret Cameron of Locheil at Corpach on 21 January 1897, with work beginning at several other sites along the line. The main construction camp at Lochailort housed 2,000 navvies at one time, with a small hospital in the old schoolhouse. Meanwhile at Loch Eil, a number of piers were specially constructed to allow the contractor's supplies to arrive by boat. It was an expensive railway to build, partly due to the number of engineering features required to cross nearly 40 miles of rugged, rocky terrain. The engineers had planned for two tunnels along the route, but it transpired that eleven had to be built in the end.

Robert McAlpine became known as 'Concrete Bob' due to his enthusiasm for using mass concrete as a construction material – a practice that was relatively unknown in the late nineteenth century. The best examples of this are the viaducts at Glenfinnan and Loch

nan Uamh, where most would agree with McAlpine's idea that the style blends in well with the scenery. Not only that, but concrete was cheaper to use than most other building materials and required less maintenance.

The navvies building the Extension faced not only a difficult job but a dangerous one at that – none more apparent than when Robert McAlpine's young son Malcolm was almost killed after being seriously injured during a routine rock blast near Lochailort. After being told by the camp doctor there that Malcolm's condition was critical, his father hastily arranged for a series of boats and a special train to be laid on to transport him southwards to a nursing home in Glasgow, where he was able to be cared for and subsequently made a full recovery.

The Mallaig Extension finally opened to traffic on 1 April 1901, some four years after construction began. Not only would it provide transport for the local community and the fishing market, it also gave the West Highland Railway their own foothold on the west coast to rival that of the Callandar & Oban Railway further south.

busy with fish traffic, the station layout has been vastly reduced, though it does still, happily, represent a busy scene when the steam-hauled 'Jacobite' shares the platform with the ScotRail service trains on a daily basis during the summer. Not only that, but Caledonian MacBrayne provide the railway with a ferry connection too, with the modern vessels MV *Coruisk* and MV *Lochnevis* plying their trade to the Isle of Skye in the case of the former, and Muck, Eigg, Rhum and Canna in the latter.

Located 164 miles from Glasgow, Mallaig marks the end of the 'Road to the Isles'. Located in an area renowned for its mild climate and spectacular sunsets, it really is a perfect bookend to the West Highland railway journey.

The Oban Line (Crianlarich–Oban)

With the closure of the line via Callander, the Oban line of today ultimately begins at Crianlarich. It would have made perfect sense for Glasgow–Oban trains to have used the line south of Crianlarich via Ardlui from the very beginning, sharing with the Glasgow–Fort William services. This was, after all, a much more direct route and it would have cut journey times immensely if Oban trains had gone this way in the days of steam. Alas, the fierce competition of the pre-nationalisation railway saw to it that this was never allowed to happen, with each of the different railway companies intent on preserving their own separate identities, going out of their way to outdo their rivals at any cost. Nowadays, Glasgow–Oban services at least benefit from this quicker journey time and it is heartening to see that the village of Crianlarich is still such an important railhead.

Leaving Crianlarich, trains take the former 'chord line' down the hill to where Crianlarich Lower Junction once stood. The line then heads through

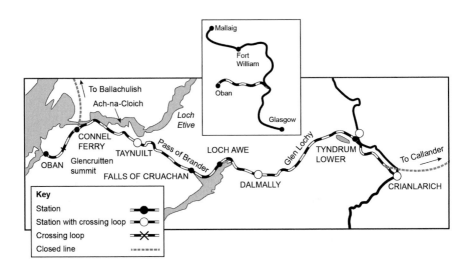

The section of line between Tyndrum Lower and Dalmally through Glen Lochy, on the route to Oban, offers a great many vantage points for photographers. On 21 January 1989, 37408 *Loch Rannoch* skirts Lochan na Bi with the 1250 Oban–Glasgow on the penultimate day of Class 37 haulage on these services. (David Webster)

Strath Fillan, taking a route along the valley floor – different to that of the Fort William route which takes a hillier course alongside the mountains at the opposite side of the valley. The Oban line takes a slight arc to cross the masonry-built Cononish Viaduct, passing the site of a recently reactivated gold mine! After lying derelict for a number of years, the extraction of gold from here is now beginning once again. Beyond here, Oban trains slow for the stop at Tyndrum Lower. Located closer to the actual village, the station here is much more accessible than Upper Tyndrum.

With the two lines parting company at Tyndrum, the Oban line proceeds to traverse almost 12 miles of uninhabited wilderness through Glen Lochy. It passes the site where a lonely signal box and passing loop were once provided at Glenlochy Crossing. The line drops downhill now, crossing Succoth Viaduct just outside Dalmally. There was famously a big celebration at this isolated spot to celebrate the viaduct's completion on a chilly November afternoon in 1876, with guests transported here on a special train. While a piper played, the revellers danced well into the evening – drinking whisky from a large cask provided on site!

As a result of Dalmally becoming the temporary terminus of the line there was a two-road engine shed located here, along with several sidings which were for

Dalmally station in 1988. (David Webster)

many years well used for transporting cattle and sheep. Still extant today is the passing loop, with a barrow crossing allowing access between the two platforms. Mercifully, the station buildings have also stood the test of time, as has the magnificent fountain with its heron-shaped plinth, carved out of granite from Ben Cruachan quarry.

Now descending towards Loch Awe – the longest freshwater loch in Scotland no less – the River Orchy is crossed on a low, lattice-girder viaduct. With the line squeezing tightly around to the northern edge of the loch, we pass the site of the former junction for a branch line that used to run up the mountains to the Ben Cruachan quarry. Closed in 1916, it transported granite from the quarry for use in building various structures on the line. About half a mile further on we reach Loch Awe station, which is most recognisable for having an old British Railways Mark 1 carriage sitting adjacent to the platform. It has been here since 1988, when it was used first as a café and then as a camping coach. The station itself was closed under the Beeching Cuts in 1965 but thankfully reopened twenty years later. The disused former Down platform is the only blight on this delightful loch-side setting.

Train travellers are also afforded a good view of the fifteenth-century-built Kilchurn Castle along this stretch: one of the most well-photographed historic structures in Scotland. The former stronghold of the Clan Campbell, its ruins stand on what is almost an island far out on the loch, which can be reached either by foot (sometimes impossible due to the level of water in the loch) or by a ferry from Lochawe village.

Still skirting the edge of the loch, the railway and A85 road twist into the Pass of Brander, where the water is reportedly as deep as the sides of the Pass are high. The first landmark in this dramatic setting is the visitor centre for Ben Cruachan power station. This popular tourist attraction houses giant turbines in a cavern half a mile below the ground, which are used to pump water from the reservoir high up on the mountain. The peak itself is 3,689ft above sea level. The wayside halt of Falls of Cruachan provides a train connection for visitors to the power station.

Sprinter 156458 threads through the Pass of Brander, with Loch Awe in the distance, 28 February 2013. (Author)

EARLY HISTORY

The original Oban line started at Dunblane, diverging from the busy Stirling–Perth main line just to the north of Dunblane station. Extending westwards through Callandar and the Trossachs, it reached temporary termini at first Tyndrum and then Dalmally, before the final section to Oban was opened on 30 June 1880 – some fourteen years before the Glasgow–Fort William route. Therefore the Callandar & Oban line, as it was known, became the first railway to reach the West Highlands. The construction of both routes was far from a simple affair, both having to adhere to tight budgets. However, the Callandar & Oban took twice as many years to build in its entirety and, unlike the West Highland, was gradually opened in stages until financial circumstances allowed it to continue.

The line from Dunblane to Callandar was built by the Dunblane, Doune & Callandar Railway, reaching the Callandar terminus in 1858, where a locomotive shed and turntable were placed. But the line didn't end there. In 1865, the Dunblane, Doune & Callandar Railway was absorbed into the Scottish Central Railway. In the same year, a new company called the Callandar & Oban Railway received royal assent to build a line westwards towards Oban. John Anderson was appointed as Secretary of the company and his influence would come to the fore later when the line reached its final stages of building towards Oban.

An entire new station was built at Callandar, with five platforms. The old station was subsequently converted into a goods yard and the line from Dunblane connected to the new one. The line continued heading in a north-westerly direction through the scenic Pass of Leny before the junction station of Balquhidder, where a line diverged eastwards towards Comrie, Crieff and Gleneagles – another link between the C&O and the Stirling–Perth main line. The line between Balquhidder and Comrie via Lochearnhead would later close in October 1951, with Balquhidder losing its junction status.

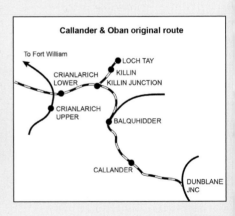

Callander & Oban original route

To Fort William

LOCH TAY

CRIANLARICH LOWER

KILLIN

KILLIN JUNCTION

CRIANLARICH UPPER

BALQUHIDDER

CALLANDER

DUNBLANE JNC

It is on this stretch of line we see the first of a number of semaphore signals planted at regular intervals, which are part of a unique trip system that was devised back in 1882 to protect the line from rockfalls on the steep slopes of Ben Cruachan. A wire screen along the side of the line is designed to activate the signals as soon as anything touches it, causing the signal arms to turn to 'danger' and warning approaching train drivers accordingly. It was brought into use after a train was hit by a boulder in 1881, and the system was conceived by the

After Balquhidder, the line headed northwards across mountainous terrain through Glen Ogle, with the railway taking a course along the edge of the hillside in a similar way to vast stretches of the nearby West Highland Line. A station was opened near here and was named after its nearby village: Killin. This formed a temporary terminus of the line, and on 1 June 1870 the line between Killin and Callandar opened to trains. Once the line was extended further this station would be closed and retained only as a passing place, becoming Glenoglehead Crossing.

Meanwhile, building of the line continued, with the railway now taking a more westerly course before reaching Killin Junction. This station was added to the line in March 1886 with the opening of a 5-mile branch line to a new Killin station. Now traversing through more gentle terrain through Glen Dochart, the line continued to another station and passing loop at Luib.

The Callandar & Oban was the first railway company to reach Crianlarich; the line leaving Luib and reaching the station here in a magnificent setting under the shadow of the towering Ben More. The station was renamed Crianlarich Lower in 1953, at the same time as the station on the West Highland Line became Crianlarich Upper. The scene here changed a great deal once the Fort William route appeared, with Crianlarich Viaduct carrying the West Highland Line over the Callandar & Oban immediately to the west of the station. Such a layout gave Crianlarich a very unique look for a countryside railway junction, with the two routes cutting across one another at right angles., The Callandar & Oban and West Highland lines were rival routes run by rival companies, but it made perfect sense to construct a chord connecting the two routes at Crianlarich, which was added a few years after the West Highland had opened in 1894.

From here the Callandar & Oban Railway Company continued to make stuttering progress in building the line westwards towards Oban and it is these further 42 miles which make up the Oban line that survives to this day. This latter stretch of line was to be no easy feat either and once again the railway had to be opened in stages. First, the stretch from Glenoglehead (Killin) to Tyndrum opened in 1873. It was almost another four years by the time it reached Dalmally on 1 April 1877.

On 30 June 1880, the railway finally reached Oban – some ten years after the first sod was cut west of Callandar.

Callander & Oban Railway secretary John Anderson. The noise of the trip wires whistling in the wind earned the system the nickname 'Anderson's Piano'.

The line now heads downhill into the village of Taynuilt – today the only other passing place on the Oban line besides Dalmally. Once-busy goods sidings are nowadays bereft of any traffic and the station itself has lost its imposing main building after it was destroyed in a fire in the 1980s. The signal box still stands, albeit boarded up and disused.

There was formerly a station a few miles further on from Taynuilt where the line starts to hug the shores of Loch Etive, called Ach-na-Cloich, where passengers used to be able to disembark for steamer cruises up Loch Etive. The station closed in the 1960s and there is not a trace of it left, save for a ruined platform. Approaching Connel Ferry there are views of Loch Etive and the Falls of Lora from the train, where the cantilever Connel Bridge crosses. Both road and rail used to famously cross this bridge – the railway being the former branch line to Ballachulish, which used to leave the main line at Connel Ferry before its closure in 1966. Since Connel Ferry lost its junction status, the station has become a shadow of its former self, with only a single platform and 'bus shelter' waiting room remaining.

The line now climbs inland for a spell to reach Oban, on a steep gradient of up to 1 in 50 to reach Glencruitten Summit. Trains coming in the opposite direction out of Oban have an equivalent climb to the top, so Glencruitten was recognised as a good spot to place a crossing loop. The large house overlooking the line here used to double as a signal box, with the levers in its front room and block bells repeated throughout the house to warn of any approaching trains. This operation ceased when the loop was removed in 1966.

Oban station, with its two-platform simplicity and disused sidings along the pier-side, is no longer the bustling seaside terminus it once was. However, the railway and Caledonian MacBrayne ferries still continue to ply their trade alongside one another, with ferry sailings to Mull and the Western Isles. It certainly makes for a most impressive sight during the summer tourist season when the two massive car ferries MV *Clansman* and MV *Isle of Mull* are berthed at the pier at the same time, alongside the train. High above the town is the famous monument known as McCaig's Tower – commissioned by wealthy local banker John Stuart McCaig as a family memorial, with the building of the structure having provided work for local stonemasons during the winter months. Oban translates in Gaelic as 'Little Bay', with its large waterfront separated from the Atlantic in the Sound of Kerrera. The last seagoing paddle steamer in the world, PS *Waverley*, also occasionally makes summer sailings out of here and together with the railway, it is hoped it will continue to serve the west coast town for some time yet.

2

Early History and Beeching

Early Days

While the North British Railway had running powers of the routes to Fort William and Mallaig, the line to Oban was operated by the Caledonian Railway. For many years the two companies had an intense rivalry, one which continued when they were absorbed into the London & North Eastern Railway (LNER) and London Midland & Scottish Railway (LMS) respectively. This continued up until nationalisation in 1948 – some say even after then. Especially interesting were the everyday scenes at Crianlarich, where the two rival companies' separate trains passed at opposite sides of the valley.

By the time the LNER and LMS took control in the 1923 grouping, several short additions had been made to the main routes. The line from Comrie joined the Callander & Oban (C&O) route at Balquidder in 1905, while the 5¼-mile branch to Killin and Loch Tay opened in 1886. The latter line would go on to survive for many years, even after the closure of Loch Tay station, where a single-road engine shed was provided.

The C&O's second branch line, Connel Ferry–Ballachulish, opened in 1903. It was 27 miles long, serving eight intermediate stations and a slate quarry and, as a result, its traffic was much heavier than that of the Killin branch. The Caledonian Railway never got their wish for a west-facing junction, though, meaning that through trains to and from Oban had to reverse at Connel Ferry. A line between Ballachulish and Fort William was also suggested; first by the Caledonian, who wanted a route running the whole way between Fort William and Connel Ferry. Then after the building of the West Highland main line, the North British proposed an extension from Fort William to Ballachulish, which also fell by the wayside.

Further east, the Spean Bridge–Fort Augustus line was opened to traffic in 1903. The North British Railway's aspirations to extend the line to Inverness proved to be nothing more than a pipe dream, though unfortunately this was not realised until after the route was constructed as far as Fort Augustus. Both the North British and Highland Railways each had a spell of running the line, but traffic diminished more and more. Astonishingly, the line had to close completely in 1911 after being open for only eight years. However, it was given a second chance and reopened by the North British in 1913.

After the grouping of the 'Big Four' railway companies in 1923, the LNER's routes to Fort William and Mallaig continued to rely heavily on the fish trains from the harbour at the latter. However, there was a dramatic increase in freight traffic after the arrival of the Lochaber aluminium smelter in 1929, which added further security to the main route to Glasgow. Both routes saw their fair share of summer tourist traffic too, helped by the many steamer connections en route. The Callander & Oban route, now operated by the LMS, also saw great summer patronage and a similarly large volume of freight carried.

The Second World War generated a great amount of freight traffic on the West Highland lines. Most significant was the opening of the double track branch line to Faslane naval base, operated by the War Department. The extra trains, many of them quite lengthy, resulted in the extension of the crossing loop at Helensburgh Upper and a new marshalling yard being built at Dalmore, near Craigendoran. The branch line diverged at Faslane Junction, where a new loop and sidings were also laid.

On the Mallaig Extension, extra sidings and loops were laid at Mallaig Junction and Corpach, where a naval base was built. Further north around Mallaig, spies and saboteurs gained training in practices such as disabling enemy locomotives and railway lines. The amount of military activity along the length of the Mallaig line involved an increased level of security too, with any potential travellers needing special authorisation to visit the area.

The Fort Augustus line had closed to passenger traffic for a second time in 1933, after it continued to fall short of expected revenue levels. It closed completely in 1946 following the cessation of goods traffic. Meanwhile the short branch to Banavie Pier was closed at the beginning of the war, on 2 September 1939, after the steamer service from the pier ceased to run.

With regards to motive power, the West Highland lines saw various classes of steam locomotive operating during the pre-war period. Lessons had been learned from the early days, when crews soon got used to the harsh weather conditions and torturous gradients, which necessitated specific types of locomotives with the suitable power, axle load and hill-climbing abilities. The heaviest passenger trains, particularly between Fort William and Glasgow, required double-heading, and the North British 'Glen' 4-4-0s became the most well established types from 1913. The 1930s saw LNER K2 and K4 moguls take over most of the work on the Fort William and Mallaig roads, with the two Gresley V4 2-6-2s also appearing in LNER days. The late 1940s would then see Thompson B1 4-6-0s start to appear on the line south of Fort William. The LMS-operated Callander & Oban line became dominated by Stanier 'Black Five' 4-6-0s following their introduction in the mid 1930s. Often double-heading, this popular class would remain the staple traction right up until the end of steam in the early 1960s. The branch lines to Killin and Ballachulish were mainly in the hands of ex-Caledonian Railway 0-4-4 tanks, supplemented by 0-6-0s such as the 'Caley Jumbos'.

Nationalisation in 1948 saw the 'Big Four' railway companies join forces to become British Railways. A regular through service from Glasgow Queen Street to Oban via Ardlui was introduced, using the chord line at Crianlarich which joined the ex-LMS and LNER routes. This was the first of many changes which would see the Oban and Fort William routes gradually moving away from their separate identities. Further evidence of this came when 'Black Fives' started to appear on the Fort William line as well, joined by the BR Standard Class 5s and further B1s from Eastfield depot. The 'Black Fives' gradually became more common as the 1950s progressed, though they steered clear of the Mallaig Extension, which was deemed unsuitable for most 4-6-0 locomotives.

The Peppercorn K1 2-6-0s were introduced to the Mallaig line from 1949 to work alongside the other ex-LNER moguls, eventually assuming a near-monopoly of both passenger and goods traffic, whilst the K4 and 'Glen' classes were seen less and less. Meanwhile, a familiar sight on the southern part of the West Highland main line was the short local service operating between Craigendoran and Arrochar, hauled by Class C15 4-4-2 tanks operating in push-pull mode. Another major feature during BR steam days was the use of observation cars at the rear of some passenger trains to Oban, Fort William and Mallaig, first introduced in 1956.

The 1960s

The fate of BR's steam locomotive fleet was sealed when the beginning of the 1960s saw new diesel and electric classes ordered in large quantities. The West Highlands was one of the first regions in Scotland to be 'dieselised', with steam engines almost completely eliminated by the end of 1962. Other areas such as Ayrshire and the central belt would see steam still running regularly until 1967. The introduction of modern traction marked the beginning of a decline on the West Highland railways that was to last throughout the 1960s, starting with the closure of steam motive power depots. Oban and Mallaig sheds closed in 1962, with Fort William becoming nothing more than a stabling point for diesels until its eventual removal too in the mid 1970s.

Dr Richard Beeching was elected to become Chairman of the new British Railways Board in 1963, which was set up to replace the British Transport Commission. He estimated that BR was operating at a loss of £140 million a year, which was a combination of two things: increased competition from road transport and lines which simply never generated enough revenue to cover their losses. His hastily produced report, *The Reshaping of British Railways*, drafted that very same year, would include a mass cull of Scottish rural lines and stations which were not paying their way. All rural branch lines fell into this category, thus the writing was on the wall for the routes to Ballachulish and Killin (the latter usually ran with just a single coach).

The main routes of the West Highlands were also recommended for closure, simply on the grounds of unprofitability, without taking into account the lack of any alternative means of transport to some of its remotest areas. While this was a good enough argument for retention of the Glasgow–Fort William–Mallaig section, the government were eventually convinced to keep the railway open after the building of the rail-connected Corpach pulp and paper mill. Scottish Pulp Developments Ltd and BR signed a contract whereby the railway would handle daily freight traffic to and from the factory. The resulting increase in goods traffic levels essentially saved the West Highland lines to Fort William and Mallaig.

Sadly, little could be done to prevent the closure of the old Callander & Oban route east of Crianlarich. BR soon recognised the importance of keeping the popular holiday destination of Oban on the railway map, though with Beeching keen to strip the railway network down to the bare minimum, there was no need to retain the Crianlarich–Dunblane section. Trains for Oban would simply be segued into the main West Highland timetable, using the Glasgow–Fort William line south of Crianlarich. Callander would lose its rail link, including its local services to Stirling and Glasgow, though the line's closure would at least safeguard the future of the Crianlarich–Oban section for the time being. Closure of the Crianlarich–Dunblane route, together with the Killin branch, was duly planned for 1 November 1965.

Rationalisation south of Crianlarich saw the closure of a number of stations, as the local trains between Arrochar and Craigendoran were dispensed with – a service which latterly employed a four-wheel diesel railbus. Rhu, Shandon, Whistlefield and the unofficial halt at Glen Douglas were the casualties, while Craigendoran lost its West Highland platform. The latter two locations would, however, retain crossing loops and their signal boxes. Craigendoran was an especially interesting location, as by this time the main line between Glasgow and Helensburgh Central was electrified.

With closure of the Callander & Oban route imminent, a landslide in Glen Ogle resulted in the line west of Callander being shut prematurely, on 28 September 1965. This curious occurrence, which saw the line blocked by fallen rocks between Balquhidder and Killin Junction, is believed by many to have been a deliberate act to ensure the line's closure. However, the truth of this will never be known and the story has gone down in West Highland railway folklore. BR operated a replacement bus service until the official closure date on 1 November, when the line between Callander and Dunblane also saw its last trains.

This April 1968 photograph shows the approach to the old Fort William station alongside Loch Linnhe. A Class 29 can be seen ready to attach the stock of the 1300 ex-Mallaig to the sleeping cars from London, to form the 1615 Fort William–Glasgow Queen Street. Another NBL Type 2 can just be discerned in the distance alongside the station platforms. (Allan Trotter, Eastbank Model Railway Club)

The Killin branch had shut on 28 September after losing its main line connection, remaining steam-hauled by BR Standard 2-6-4 tanks until the very end despite dieselisation to Oban. The Ballachulish line managed to hold on until 28 March 1966, failing to survive the Beeching Axe despite the successful introduction of BRCW (Birmingham Railway Carriage and Wagon Company) Class 27 diesels in common with the main line services. Track lifting took place promptly, along with the Callander & Oban route, though plenty of old railway infrastructure would still be evident in the area for years to come, not least the Connel Bridge, which still carried road traffic.

The Crianlarich–Oban section of line would also see significant rationalisation. Loch Awe, Falls of Cruachan and Ach-na-Cloich stations were all closed between 1965–66. The remote crossing loops on the line at Glenlochy, Loch Awe, Awe Crossing (in the Pass of Brander) and Glencruitten Summit were also removed together with their associated signal boxes, in further cost-cutting measures during 1966. Another piece of Callander & Oban Railway history was wiped out when Glasgow Buchanan Street station closed its doors for the final time on 7 November 1966, being deemed surplus to requirements following the Beeching Report. Oban trains had switched to operating out of Glasgow Queen Street a year previously following the closure of the route through Callander.

A view from the window of a typical West Highland passenger service in the aftermath of Beeching. The 0600 Glasgow Queen Street–Fort William nears the Monessie Gorge with an NBL Type 2 in charge, during April 1968. As well as two through sleeping cars from London Kings Cross, there is a buffet-restaurant car and an ex-Southern Railway PMV parcels van in the eight-vehicle formation. (Allan Trotter, Eastbank Model Railway Club)

The year 1967 saw Connel Ferry station become a mere shadow of its former self following the closure of the Ballachulish branch; reduced to just a single platform after the removal of both signal boxes and all associated pointwork. However, it did become something of an important railhead again a year later, when a new Shell oil storage depot was built adjacent to the platform. It was rail-connected, and both sidings and a run-round loop were installed, controlled by ground frames. Oil traffic would feature heavily over the Oban line over the next couple of decades as a result. Two years later, Tyndrum Lower would also lose its crossing loop and signal box.

The Fort William and Mallaig routes got through the 1960s relatively unscathed in comparison. The volume of freight carried south of Fort William ensured that most crossing loops would stay in place. The new traffic from the Wiggins Teape paper mill at Corpach played a big part, as did the aluminium smelter, with further traffic obtained from the similar plant at Kinlochleven (formerly carried over the Ballachulish branch). However, these new flows coincided with the complete loss of the fish traffic to Mallaig, something which itself had kept the railway open for a long time. This was now transported by road.

Lochailort was one of the few locations which did lose its signal box and crossing loop. It became a simple, unstaffed, single-platform affair, as did Roy Bridge on the main line to Glasgow, both of these changes happening during 1966. Helensburgh Upper lost its loop in 1968.

3

The British Rail Era

The start of the 1970s marked the beginning of a new era for the West Highland lines. Most notably, the Glasgow–Fort William/Mallaig and Crianlarich–Oban routes started to be regarded as the same entity, following the closure of the Oban line's original approach via Callander. Indeed from 1973, BR began marketing both under the same banner of the 'West Highland lines'. And the loss of the Callander & Oban was the Fort William line's gain. The number of trains working south of Crianlarich was virtually doubled, ensuring that the many signal boxes and crossing loops on these parts were retained for the time being. It also helped the existing railway to stave off the threat of closure.

Freight traffic was particularly healthy, with one of the most notable workings being the daily timber train operating between Crianlarich and Corpach pulp mill. Sidings had been retained on the site of the former Crianlarich Lower station and these were used as the base for loading timber from lorries. The northbound loaded working was always a heavy train and became a regular diagram for a single Class 27 diesel. There were also still freight trains which operated during the night, famous since the early days of the West Highland main line, known as the 'Ghosts'. Up to three still ran in each direction per night, serving both Oban and Fort William.

It was the Class 27s which had a monopoly of both freight and passenger services in the West Highlands throughout the 1970s, becoming more prolific after the last of the troublesome NBL Type 2s were withdrawn from BR stock. By the beginning of the decade, virtually all diesel locomotives had been repainted using BR's 'corporate blue' livery, with coaching stock in blue and grey colours to match. This was part of BR's new image implemented after Beeching, under the new banner of 'British Rail'. By contrast, operating practices and infrastructure along the lines remained in much the same fashion as they had in steam days and it was to largely remain this way throughout the 1970s.

The diesels still had two train-crew members in the cab, with one of the secondman's duties being the exchanging of the single line token at passing places. And the old West Highland tradition of double-heading continued on some of the heavier trains in a throwback to the early days of steam. This was especially so on the Fort William–London Kings Cross overnight sleeper, as it could load up to nine or ten coaches. Though the impressive horsepower of the Class 27s meant that pairing locomotives was no longer a necessity.

Summer observation cars had disappeared from the West Highlands. They were formerly able to be positioned facing out from the rear of the train in both directions of travel, though the ability to do this was lost with the removal of steam locomotive turntables. However, Crianlarich Upper, now named simply 'Crianlarich' after closure of the Lower station, retained its famous tea room housed in the station building – a feature here since the early days of the railway.

One major change to services on the Extension came early in 1973, when Mallaig lost its Stornoway ferry service. A more direct crossing was established, operating out of a new terminal at Ullapool – eliminating the previous lengthy journey from Mallaig via Kyle of Lochalsh. While Mallaig had a railway link, Ullapool could only be reached by road and this was a clear example of the

The second Fort William station was still fairly new when this shot was taken in June 1980, with Class 25 No 25006 at the head of a train for Glasgow. This particular locomotive was one of several 25s seen fairly regularly on the West Highland lines between 1975 and 1980 and could be easily distinguished by the dent visible above its buffer beam.

A ride south behind the Class 25 pictured above allowed the photographer the chance to catch this passing unidentified Class 27 at Crianlarich, with an oil train bound for Connel Ferry. Note the secondman preparing to hand over the single-line token. (Both Allan Trotter, Eastbank Model Railway Club)

gradual changes in tourism habits around this time: the move from trains to cars. However, for some years to come, it was still possible to catch a summer-only ferry between Mallaig and Kyle of Lochalsh. This was a journey taking around two hours, linking two of Western Scotland's classic seaside railway terminuses.

Since the abolition of fish traffic in the 1960s, Mallaig had been left with little freight. The only regular flow was oil, used by various fishing vessels operating out of the harbour. Rather than running a separate train, it was decided that it would be more convenient to convey the tankers (typically a rake of three) on the back of passenger trains and shunt them to and from the small terminal adjacent to Mallaig station. Any other odd goods wagon required would often also be part of the service train – resulting in mixed workings with coaches, wagons and a brake van!

West Highland services remained well-patronaged for most of the 1970s, particularly during the summer, with longer train lengths as a result. Bus services in the Highlands were still limited and for many the railway was the most, and sometimes the only, accessible method of transport, particularly during the winter. But despite the competition between the railway and the bus companies, they worked well with one another. Buses connected with trains to allow continued travel to some of the other villages in the Highlands which were not (or no longer) rail-connected, such as Ballachulish, Fort Augustus and Kinlochleven. Indeed one of the abiding memories of the old station at Fort William was the green, cream and red colours of MacBrayne's coaches, who operated a number of services from the pier alongside the trains.

The original Fort William station had a very cramped layout and over the years this had become an operational nightmare at times, especially on busy summer Saturdays, with up to three trains occupying the platforms at once. Three platform roads were provided, though these frequently proved to be not long enough. The platform alongside the sea wall was longer than the other two, so this tended to be used the most.

A lengthy train would often foul the points at the station throat and prevent other movements to and from the platforms. There was also no siding space at the terminus. The move to diesel power and the abolishment of fish traffic had simplified operating procedures slightly, but the one existing crossover had been removed, eliminating locomotive run-rounds. An incoming service was usually taken back out on its return journey by another locomotive at the Mallaig end of the station, allowing the locomotive at the buffer stop to be released.

Expansion of Fort William station was never possible thanks to its location, with the edge of Loch Linnhe at one side and the town centre on the other. This also blocked off Loch Linnhe from the town. Eventually it was decided that a better option was to build an all-new station to the eastern side of the town, which would also allow for a dual-carriageway bypass road to be built on the

LIFE ALONG THE RAILWAY

There have been many stories over the years about the way the West Highland railways played a massive part in people's everyday lives. In particular, many remote settlements along the length of the line were far away from the main road, or any other kind of civilisation for that matter. Ever since the early days of the railway, passing footplate crews would happily fetch the shopping for the locals when they reached Glasgow or Fort William and bring it up on the train. These practices continued well into the diesel era.

During the 1970s, one particular resident who stayed in a house next to the line between Arrochar and Ardlui, used to have her shopping dropped off from the passing train every Thursday – and left the train crew some home baking in return! Another story is of a lady who lived in a former surfaceman's cottage in the desolate mountainside terrain around the Horseshoe Curve. The morning train to Glasgow would stop along the edge of the glen, where she would board it using a ladder. After getting her shopping in Glasgow she would be dropped back home on a return working later in the day.

West Highland railwaymen, past and present, have always been well-known for their friendly nature and such gestures were testament to this. But this did not stop passengers from further afield taking liberties. One occasion saw a passenger at Glasgow Queen Street, on crutches and with their leg in plaster, make a request to the driver to stop the train a mile to the north of Corrour to allow him a quicker route to the nearby shooting lodge. The sympathetic driver duly stopped at this spot, only for the now crutch-less passenger to make a run across the moor, along with a dozen more companions spilling out of the coach.

Locomotive crews would enjoy the native cuisine, in much the same way as passengers. One particular driver spoke of a mini-grill that used to be carried in the cab of the Class 27s, used to cook locally-cured kippers during layover at Oban! But even this pales in comparison to a story of another BR footplateman, who, on a trip returning from Fort William to Glasgow, came across a dead stag which had unfortunately been hit by a train earlier in the day. Using the opportunity to his full advantage, the driver took it home and cooked it for his dinner!

site of the old station and its erstwhile signal box. The new Fort William station opened on 13 June 1975, incorporating a lengthy island platform, run-round loop and two adjacent sidings. It was located closer to Mallaig Junction, with the result that the existing short length of track towards the old station was lifted.

The goods yard and former motive power depot were lost with the old station approach line and this was the catalyst for the building of a new depot at Tom-na-Faire, on the outskirts of the town, during the summer of 1975. Situated just beyond Mallaig Junction at the beginning of the Extension line and covering a previously unoccupied site of open meadows, it would be used for the stabling of locomotives, coaches, wagons and other rolling stock. Tom-na-Faire was linked to the adjacent loop sidings of Mallaig Junction Yard and boasted a locomotive shed and fuelling point. Its multipurpose nature meant that all sorts of railway paraphernalia was typically seen here through the years, including the resident snowploughs and tool van.

Photographs taken on the West Highland lines during the days of steam depict a landscape of open mountainous terrain virtually devoid of heavy vegetation or forestry. By the 1970s, line-side vegetation began growing substantially, while many sections of hillside, formerly bare, were taken over for forestry plantations. By the early 1980s, the scene already looked vastly different, with huge acres of land now covered with conifer trees. The Glen Falloch–Strath Fillan section was a prime example. Other plantations around Glen Lochy and Tulloch were in their infancy at this time, but a quick look at the same spots today will reveal blanket forestry. This growth in the timber industry at the time was evident all over the Highlands and Argyllshire in particular.

Despite this, Wiggins Teape closed its pulp-making facility at Corpach in October 1980 for economic reasons, though the paper mill remained open. The daily timber train from Crianlarich ceased to operate as a result, following the final working on 9 June 1980. Though Corpach still received daily freight traffic, with pulp and china clay coming in by train and finished paper going out. Meanwhile, Taynuilt and Arrochar were established as new timber-loading bases in addition to that at Crianlarich, with the surrounding hillsides providing a healthy supply of logs now carried to various destinations in the south.

The following year, 1981, saw the Faslane Military Railway also close. It had continued to exist after the war, still shrouded in complete secrecy, with very occasional trains still serving it throughout the 1970s. Little is known today of these mysterious trains, though it is known that they were goods workings conveying scrap metal from the ship-breaking activities on the Gare Loch and usually hauled by Class 20s. By this time, access to the line was controlled by a ground frame at Faslane Junction on the main line.

In 1980, Class 37s begin to make regular appearances on the West Highland lines, replacing Class 27s on both passenger and freight trains over the next couple of years. A significant amount of track maintenance took place in anticipation of this, with the heavier English Electric locomotives not quite designed for the permanent way in this part of the country as their predecessors were (there were parallels of this many years later when Class 37s were in turn replaced by Class 66s). But the hostile terrain provided obstacles for any engine and as well as the gradients and curves, mother nature played its part. Sheep and, in particular, deer have always roamed free around the Fort William and Mallaig lines and unfortunately they still collide with trains to this day. Inclement weather

1981 saw Class 37s take over West Highland passenger services. Ben Nevis towers in the background, as split-headcode 37037 approaches Banavie with the 1405 Fort William–Mallaig on 14 May 1985. It is pleasing to report that the locomotive lives on today in preservation, based at the North Norfolk Railway and carrying its original identity of D6737. It was renumbered for a period in the late 1980s as 37321. (Bob Avery)

has always been a problem too, not just snow, but with the West Highland lines experiencing fallen trees, flooding and landslides. The early part of January 1981 saw a landslip block the Oban line between Dalmally and Taynuilt for nearly three days, while early March the following year saw flooding at Craigendoran.

On 28 August 1982, a northbound freight train hauled by Class 37 No 37018 derailed at Blairvadach Farm, between Rhu and Garelochhead. Several wagons, conveying china clay and petrol, were thrown on to their sides into the adjacent field. The Fire Brigade then arrived to promptly dig a ditch to be filled with foam, to stop petrol leakages from the wagons reaching the nearby houses.

The often-overlooked 1983 *Serpell Report* was commissioned by the Tory government to examine the viability of the current BR network and suggest major changes as a result. This was anticipated to perhaps follow a similar pattern to Beeching, with a possible outcome being the loss of most secondary routes in the country. Especially worrying was the sharp decline in passenger train revenue since the 1960s, though this was no worse in the West Highlands than anywhere else.

A proposal was made to close the lines north and west of Crianlarich. This strange move was met with fierce opposition, led by the Friends of the

Superpower for a three-coach train! The crisp winter's morning of 14 February 1987 sees 37079 and 37405 *Strathclyde Region* in charge of the 0950 Glasgow–Fort William at the top of Glen Falloch. The leading locomotive was only based in Scotland for a few months of its working life, allocated to Eastfield depot. It piloted this train as far as Crianlarich only – the reasons for which are unknown. (David Webster)

West Highland Lines (FoWHL), a group newly formed to promote the railway. In the end, common sense prevailed and the government decided against making any cutbacks. Though the report did spark changes in BR's organisational structure, one of which saw the Scottish Region taken over by new management to become ScotRail.

It was clear that if the West Highland lines were to survive, it would take something more imaginative than the present provision of services. Little had been done to promote tourism until 1980, when an observation car was reintroduced on the afternoon Fort William–Mallaig return service for the summer season. Its success prompted ScotRail to explore further avenues of attracting passengers to the railway. This included 'Summer Sunday' excursions, which were introduced in July 1983 as through workings between Edinburgh and Oban. BR had tried this out before during the summer of 1981, with a 'Deltic' diesel hauling a rake of air-conditioned Mark 2 and Mark 3 carriages usually employed on Glasgow–Edinburgh push-pull services. This time the motive power would not be as exotic, but the new excursions once again used a push-pull rake, which would otherwise have been unused on that particular day of the week.

The use of the air-conditioned stock was an inspired idea from ScotRail, providing superb InterCity-style comfort ideal for the scenic views out to Oban. After the first couple of runs it proved to be a real hit and the following excursions, running until September, ran fully booked. The trains were advertised in the public timetable too, unlike the runs two years previously, and were open to ordinary ticket holders. On board, a running commentary provided a description of the route, while hostesses sold various gifts branded with the 'Scottie Dog' emblem to promote the West Highland lines.

While Class 37s provided the motive power, the Summer Sunday trains were the first in the country to use ETHELs (Electric Train Heating Ex-Locomotives). These were former Class 25 diesels passed into departmental stock for use as mobile train heat generators. The three machines – named *ETHEL 1, 2* and *3* respectively – were converted for this purpose in late 1982. This involved isolating their traction motors, making them unable to move under their own power, and a repaint in BR blue and grey livery to match the coaching stock. On the trains in question, an ETHEL was positioned behind the '37' in both directions, in fact to provide air conditioning for the stock instead of heat at that time of year.

The reason for the creation of the ETHELs was to provide heat for the Fort William–London Euston sleeper service. BR's sleepers required to be modernised, with a switch from steam heat Mark 1 stock to electric heat Mark 3s. However, there were no Class 37s in the country fitted with Electric Train Heating (ETH) and the only diesel classes that were, such as Class 47s, had too heavy an axle load to work the line to Fort William. Speculation mounted that the West Highland would lose its sleeper service as a result of this, but thankfully the idea of ETHELs was conceived. October 1983 saw the three units introduced on the sleeper, together with the new coaching stock, while the aforementioned excursion traffic to Oban had given BR the chance to test them in advance of this.

Sunday trains had hitherto been nonexistent to Oban, Fort William and Mallaig. However, 1983 saw services offered between Fort William and Mallaig every Sunday during August (twice in each direction), again on an 'excursion' basis but without the air-conditioned stock used to Oban. These operations also proved profitable and allowed ScotRail to test the waters for regular Sunday trains in the future.

Prior to the creation of ScotRail, BR had made some effort to increase the Mallaig Extension's potential for tourism, when an observation car returned for the summer of 1980 – the first time since 1967. This was referred to in the BR timetable as a 'saloon car', with a conductor providing a running commentary about the railway. This initiative also proved popular with passengers, so it was

THE WEST HIGHLAND TERRIER

Otherwise known as the 'Westie' or 'Scottie Dog', the West Highland Terrier motif was originally conceived when Eastfield Traction Maintenance Depot decided to inject a bit of personalisation to their locomotive fleet, all of which carried the monotonous BR 'corporate blue' colour scheme. After a few livery variations on their Class 37 fleet, the 'Scottie Dog' was soon adopted on the body-sides of many locomotives. Initially it was just the 37s which carried it, but the depot later applied it to most other resident classes too.

Interestingly, the motifs started off very small in size but soon got bigger! BR was gradually beginning to accept such changes after a very long period of enforcing 'corporate blue' on virtually all rolling stock and the staff at Eastfield were undoubtedly a driving force behind the mass livery variations that followed in the latter years of BR. Eastfield was one of the first depots to have its own mascot of this sort, which was soon followed by many more across the BR network, such as the Inverness 'Highland Stag' and Stratford 'Cockney Sparrow'.

The 'Scottie Dog' later appeared in the form of metal diamond-shaped depot plaques applied to locomotives, especially those in Railfreight colours. It largely disappeared following privatisation, though many attempts have been made to revive it in recent years. Some Class 37s received the emblems during their twilight days on the West Highland lines, as well as more alien traction such as the 'Deltics' that visited on a 2003 railtour. Often these were simply very small stickers applied around the cab area, noted on Class 66s and at least one Class 156 (156492).

The 'Scottie Dog' was of course also used as a general symbol for the West Highland lines during the early days of the ScotRail sector in the 1980s. It turned out to be a popular marketing initiative and soon appeared everywhere. 'Black Five' No 5407 was adorned with a cab-side motif at one point, along with all of the coaching stock used on the summer steam excursions. The 'Scottie Dog' also appeared on various publicity material associated with the lines and most station nameboards (see left). Even the Fort William snowplough had one!

continued for the next couple of summers too. Another observation car was introduced in 1983; the train now being equipped with one at each end and providing for the first time a view in either direction. It was conveyed on the afternoon train from Fort William and return.

But the image of beautiful summer sunshine and bustling tourist traffic still contrasted vividly with wintertime in the Highlands. Heavy blizzards in January 1984 saw the main line to Glasgow completely blocked by snowdrifts for four days, with one passenger train getting stuck around County March Summit. Pairs of Class 37s were sandwiched between independent snowploughs to clear the line round the clock, where the crews encountered even more difficulties. One locomotive ended up derailing on Rannoch Moor after running over its own multiple-working jumper cable, after the classmate it was paired with had also failed. Their cab-side doors had also been frozen shut, forcing the crews to break in/out using the locomotives' nose-end doors! Eventually the snow subsided, but not until supplies in Fort William and Oban had started running low after four days without any trains.

The summer of 1984 saw a watershed moment in recent history of the West Highland lines. The success of the Sunday excursions over the Mallaig Extension operated the previous year saw this programme repeated for the duration of the summer, with extra trains also pencilled in for selected weekdays too. But it was the motive power for these trains which really caught the public's imagination. Class 37s were to be expected of course, but what about LMS 'Black Fives' and an LNER J36 0-6-0? Steam trains were back with a vengeance to the West Highlands for the first time in over twenty years, with regular trains advertised for haulage by preserved Class 5s Nos 5407 and 44767 and North British Railway No 673 *Maude*. And what's more, they were essentially service trains operated by BR and advertised in the public timetable (albeit with a supplementary fare charged).

The operations are examined in detail later in this book but to cut a long story short, the steam trains were an incredible success. Running three days a week, they were used by over 11,000 passengers and this boosted summer passenger revenue on the Mallaig Extension by around 20 per cent. Helped by some scorching weather that particular year, the steam excursions gave the Mallaig Extension a new lease of life. Just prior to this the future had looked rather ominous for the line, with station buildings falling into disrepair, no freight trains west of Corpach and various cutbacks, such as 'one train working' implemented between Arisaig and Mallaig.

Prospects were further improved for the Mallaig line when the new Loch Eil Outward Bound station was opened on 20 April 1985. The Oban line also received a boost when Loch Awe station was reopened on 10 May that year, with connecting boat cruises to Kilchurn Castle available once again. Both examples showed ScotRail's commitment to promoting tourism on the West Highland lines.

Closed under Beeching but subsequently reopened in 1985, Loch Awe station is seen on 17 October 1987, with 37413 *Loch Eil Outward Bound* hauling the 0820 Glasgow–Oban. The locomotive's name was previously carried by 37111, pictured on page 89. (David Webster)

This was further exemplified when a Class 104 DMU was employed to work a summer-only shuttle service between Oban and Crianlarich, where it provided useful connections with trains to and from Fort William. The multiple unit was painted in a special maroon and white livery advertising the Scottish Tourist Board, which gained it the nickname 'The Mexican Bean'.

The 'Mexican Bean' and an ETHEL were amongst the attractions at an open day held at Oban station on the weekend of 11–12 May 1985, attracting large crowds in good weather. It also saw Class 37 No 37188 receive the name *Jimmy Shand*. There was an observation car used on the Oban–Glasgow circuit during the summer of 1985, though there was no longer one provided to Mallaig. Attention was turned mostly to the steam excursions, which returned to the Extension once again following the success of their first season. Now running five days a week, they would continue to be a regular fixture over the following few years too.

While the 1980s had so far been a very prosperous decade for the West Highland lines, development of a different kind began to take hold. Adoption of RETB (Radio Electronic Token Block) signalling would allow BR to slash costs significantly; this equipment had already proved to be successful on rural lines after its recent launch on the Inverness–Kyle of Lochalsh/Wick/Thurso routes. Nearly all of the remaining signal boxes serving the West Highland routes (sixteen in total) and their associated signalmen would be made redundant, to be replaced by a new signalling centre at Banavie. Here, all train movements over the three lines would be controlled by two operators, communicating with drivers via radio.

A couple of crew members have a chat alongside a very imposing looking 37014 at Fort William on 2 August 1986, at the head of an Edinburgh–Mallaig SRPS railtour. The train was steam-hauled from Fort William to Mallaig and back behind 'Black Five' No 44767 *George Stephenson*. (David Webster)

Ever since the early days of the railway, semaphore signals had been a familiar sight along its entire length. Most were removed between late 1985 and 1986 in anticipation of RETB, with loop points converted to automatic, spring-loaded operation, though signalmen still remained to exchange the single track tokens until the new system was commissioned. RETB was inaugurated on the Mallaig Extension on 7 December 1987, followed by the Helensburgh Upper–Crianlarich–Oban section on 27 March 1988. The new Banavie signalling centre was officially opened on 19 May 1988 before the final part between Mallaig Junction and Crianlarich was converted on 28 May 1988.

The Intercity 'West Highlander' land cruise began using steam haulage between Fort William and Mallaig in the summer of 1987. 'Black Five' No 5305 *Alderman A.E. Draper* is captured heading the train past the western end of Loch Eilt on Sunday 24 May 1987, as the 1000 Fort William–Mallaig. These excursions utilised the same green and cream set of coaches used on the regular steam workings. (Tom Noble)

Following this, all signal boxes were taken out of use, with the exception of two. Annat box, near Corpach, was retained to control two nearby level crossings. Mallaig Junction box also survived to control Fort William station and the nearby yards, though it was renamed Fort William Junction to avoid confusion in radio messages. Semaphores still stood at both locations, as well as at the Pass of Brander, where the special 'Anderson's Piano' system was unaffected by RETB (see chapter one). The removal of signals elsewhere did not happen overnight though, with many posts still remaining in place for some time, while some 'arms' lay dumped at the side of the line awaiting uplift.

The closure of signal boxes meant that most West Highland stations now became unstaffed and sadly the condition of most of them would gradually start to deteriorate as a result. However, the main buildings at Rannoch and Bridge of Orchy also served as local post offices and a member of staff still remained at these locations for a few years after.

The summer of 1987 had seen the long single track section between Bridge of Orchy and Rannoch broken up by the reinstallation of Gorton crossing loop. The loop had closed following Beeching but was rebuilt mainly for the benefit of the permanent way department. Meanwhile on the Oban line, Falls of Cruachan station was reopened on 20 June 1988, having been originally closed in 1965. This summer-only request stop was provided to cater for hikers climbing Ben Cruachan and for visitors to the adjacent visitor centre, reached via the new footpath running down the hill to the A85 road.

Unfortunately, though, the 'Mexican Bean' did not call at the new station, the DMU shuttle service being withdrawn after the 1987 summer season. DMUs would soon become commonplace, however, with locomotive-hauled trains due to be replaced imminently by Sprinter units. In 1988 the first driver training runs commenced with the Class 156s, and diesel enthusiasts flocked to the Highlands to capture the last few months of Class 37 haulage.

The changeover from loco-haulage to Sprinters was quick and seamless, with no fuss or fond farewell for the English Electric Type 3s, though they would still continue to make everyday appearances hauling freight, for charters and with the Euston sleeper. It really was a new era for the West Highland lines, not just with the change in rolling stock but the timetabling too, which was changed significantly following the Sprinters' introduction on 23 January 1989.

The new era was briefly interrupted in March 1989 when heavy rainfall caused a culvert to be washed away on Rannoch Moor, temporarily severing the main line between Rannoch and Bridge of Orchy and derailing a passing freight train. A new, short section of track had to be laid, slewed around the spot where the accident happened and with a temporary speed restriction in place.

The introduction of Class 156s was the final step in BR's 1980s cost-cutting exercises, with the West Highland lines now taking a more settled appearance

A view from the window crossing Rannoch Viaduct, with Class 37 No 37424 hauling a very late-running SRPS railtour from Edinburgh on 9 December 1989. The train had been severely delayed at Helensburgh Upper, where problems with the RETB signalling forced the driver to find a nearby payphone to obtain a fresh token north! (David Webster)

as the end of the decade approached. Bright marketing campaigns and the introduction of the Fort William–Mallaig steam operations had resulted in a vast increase in passenger revenue, which brought back memories of the golden era of the 1950s and 1960s. Seemingly dilapidated and tired-looking for much of the 1970s, the railway looked revived and rejuvenated under the stewardship of ScotRail. The creation of this new sector of BR clearly worked, giving the entire Scottish network its own brand and unique identity which stood out from all the rest, and lines all across the country were benefiting from it. Could this be a sign of things to come?

4

From British Rail to First ScotRail

The West Highland railway scene during the early 1990s was one dominated by summer tourism and excursion traffic. BR's Sprinter units running over the Mallaig Extension seemed virtually insignificant next to the steam-hauled trains, which were by now a vital part of the economy in Lochaber. And there were no less than three different luxury land cruise trains in operation to Oban,

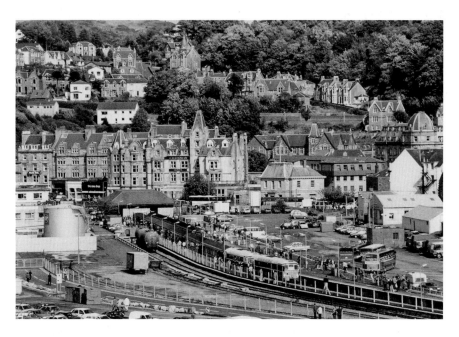

A panoramic view of Oban station with a crowded scene on the platforms, as celebrity BR green Class 26 duo D5300 (26007) and D5301 (26001) wait to leave with a ScotRail special to Edinburgh, alongside a four-car Sprinter. Note the BP oil depot, which would soon lose its rail traffic not long after this picture was taken on 21 August 1992. (Jules Hathaway)

Fort William and Mallaig. The privately-owned 'Royal Scotsman' commenced running in 1985 and was soon followed by the more affordable, InterCity-operated 'West Highlander'. The year 1990 then saw appearances of the 'Queen of Scots' pullman, utilising the vintage rolling stock formerly used on the 'Royal Scotsman'. And all these were regular timetabled trains too – the 'West Highlander' itself made thirteen different tours between April and October 1990.

On 10 April 1991, the evening Oban–Glasgow service collided head-on with Class 37 No 37405 *Strathclyde Region* at Craigendoran Junction, injuring both the crew and seven passengers. *Strathclyde Region* had been waiting in the passing loop with a northbound freight when the Sprinter was wrongly routed onto the same line. This was caused by a signal cable which had been renewed and wired incorrectly. While the 37 was eventually repaired at Springburn Works, the leading coach of Sprinter 156456 had to be written off.

The introduction of RETB (see chapter three) and Sprinters on the West Highland lines had made things much smoother from an operational point of view, and less costly, although the Sprinters were never fully accepted by passengers for a number of reasons. A common complaint was about their lack of space, in particular they had a limited amount of seating and poor capacity for luggage and bicycles compared to loco-hauled trains. Fans of loco-haulage were also unhappy with the opening droplight windows on coaching stock being replaced by the hopper-type versions on Sprinters, as it is not possible to hang out of these!

It must be remembered that despite all of the criticism, the Class 156s were actually one of the most successful of BR's 'Second Generation' DMUs. But summer overcrowding on the West Highland lines became a problem, especially with a lack of extra units available to strengthen services. As a result, and to serve as a morale booster, ScotRail agreed to bring back Class 37-hauled trains for selected summer services, utilising spacious Mark 2 coaching stock. ScotRail branded the trains 'Young Explorers', and marketed them specifically with hillwalkers and climbers in mind.

The 'Young Explorers' (latterly shortened to 'Explorers') were in operation each summer from 1992–94, running Monday–Saturday. For the first year, the operations were centred on the Fort William and Mallaig lines only, including three return trips to Mallaig each day. 1993 saw one out and back working between Fort William and Glasgow Queen Street only, but it was expanded again in 1994 to include Oban. This was a Glasgow–Oban return on Mondays, Fridays and Saturdays only and Glasgow–Fort William on the remaining days. Unfortunately, the loco-hauled trains did not run on all of the days they were supposed to operate that summer due to signalling strikes, particularly services to Oban.

August 1994 marked the centenary of the West Highland main line. As well as various civic celebrations on the day, 7 August saw the Scottish Railway

Preservation Society (SRPS) run a special double-headed steam excursion using LNER K4 No 3442 *The Great Marquess* and K1 No 2005 from Edinburgh to Fort William. The train ended up running 3½ hours late due to a multitude of problems; chiefly RETB faults and being held behind a late-running northbound sleeper. On 11 August – 100 years to the day of the line's opening ceremony – there was another special diesel-hauled to Fort William, before *The Great Marquess* hauled a single carriage under a specially-constructed archway to re-enact the scenes of the original 1894 celebrations.

The privatisation of BR could well have seen the loss of the summer steam train to Mallaig but thankfully the new Carnforth-based operator, the West Coast Railway Company, stepped in to continue the operation, which was now renamed 'The Jacobite' for the 1995 season. Though the loss of BR did preclude a return for the 'Young Explorers', mainly due to the high costs of leasing the rolling stock. The 'West Highlander' tours also ceased to operate, leaving the West Highland lines dominated by Sprinters.

The West Highlands very nearly lost its overnight sleeper service too. Expansion of the service earlier in the decade had seen it begin operating seven days a week with a new Saturday working, in addition to now conveying Motorail vans.

The new-look Fort William–Mallaig steam service, named 'The Jacobite', was launched in 1995. BR Standard Class 4MT No 75014 is caught on camera near Fassfern, on the shores of Loch Eil, with a Mallaig-bound working on 27 June 1997. (Jules Hathaway)

However, BR argued that the Fort William–Edinburgh portion of the sleeper was running at a loss of £2.5 million per annum, with demand not high enough to justify its continued use. Their proposal to withdraw the service was met with a huge backlash, led mainly by the Friends of the West Highland Lines and the Highlands and Islands Regional Council. It even became a big political talking point, with the issue being debated in the Houses of Parliament, as local councillors and other supporters of the service highlighted the devastating social and economic impact on the West Highlands if the sleeper was axed.

Without the sleeper there would be no link between London and the West Highlands, with no available air transport. Financial experts also proved BR's operating deficit figures to be somewhat exaggerated. Nevertheless, the soon-to-be-defunct BR proposed to ditch the service on 28 May 1995, since the operation was seen to be too unviable to include in the new franchise for passenger trains in Scotland. But this was blocked thanks to a successful legal challenge by the Highlands and Islands Regional Council, and eventually the powers that be were persuaded to let the service continue, to the delight of the local community.

However, Motorail vans would no longer be carried on the sleeper, preceding its acquisition in early 1997 by the new National Express-owned ScotRail franchise,

A view of Fort William Tom-na-Faire depot on 27 June 1997, with Class 37/4s Nos 37424 and 37428 *David Lloyd George* in attendance alongside an unidentified classmate and yard shunter 08630. Also of note are the timber wagons awaiting loading, coaching stock for the 'Jacobite' and the distant bridge which carries the Fort William–Mallaig line over the River Lochy. (Jules Hathaway)

which took over operations of all passenger services on the West Highland lines. This saw the train rebranded as the 'Caledonian Sleeper', this renaming being part of some much-needed marketing initiatives by the new company. The now veteran Class 37s would continue to haul the train, although now requiring to be hired from freight operator TransRail, which was succeeded by EWS.

A derailment took place on 5 April 1997 at Milepost 52, just east of Falls of Cruachan station, when the 1810 Oban–Glasgow service struck a landslip. Passengers and crew were unhurt and the Class 156 unit involved remained upright after impact. It turned out that soil and glacial matter had been washed on to the track following a rainstorm, managing to slip undetected underneath the wire screen which activates the 'Anderson's Piano' stone signals. It was the first derailment here since August 1946. The accident showed that all these years later the rockfall protection system was still necessary, even though it was unable to detect this particular landslide.

For the first time since the 1980s, ScotRail started to be seen more as a unique brand as the new millennium took hold. The colourful new white/purple/green/terracotta livery set Scotland's trains apart from the rest and was soon applied to all of the West Highland Sprinter fleet. The 'Caledonian Sleeper' also became a brand in its own right; the rolling stock being repainted in a bright new purple livery to finally escape the clutches of the old InterCity era.

This era also saw both freight and passenger operators replacing their life-expired ex-BR locomotives and rolling stock with more modern equivalents. These changes were afoot all over Scotland, though the West Highlands were largely unaffected at this early stage. Class 158 'Express' DMUs replaced Class 156s on the Inverness–Kyle of Lochalsh/Wick/Thurso routes during 2000, but there were no plans to introduce them to Glasgow–Oban/Fort William/Mallaig, the biggest difficulty being that their outward-swinging automatic doors would foul the platform edges. ScotRail's newly introduced Class 170 'Turbostar' units would also steer clear of the West Highlands due to route availability issues. Evidently there seemed to be no immediate plans to replace the 156s, which by this time had extra bicycle and luggage space added.

Railtrack and EWS spent an estimated £300,000 to assess and upgrade a number of underbridges on the Glasgow–Fort William line to enable new Class 66 diesels to operate, replacing Class 37s on freight workings from September 2000. This highlighted EWS's commitment to their West Highland traffic, which they must have expected to flourish for some time to come. Unfortunately though, by this time the big two customers at the centre of the line's overall freight operations were questioning the future of using rail transport. Arjo Wiggins (formerly Wiggins Teape) were experiencing a downturn in demand for finished products from their Corpach paper mill, partly thanks to the adoption of 'chip and pin' technology, and deemed it more viable to use road

37409 *Loch Awe* powers the 0505 Edinburgh–Fort William portion of the London Euston sleeper near Milepost 50, north of Bridge of Orchy, on 17 June 1999. Proposals to axe the service in 1995 were quashed. (Jules Hathaway)

transport for the remaining goods. Alcan (formerly British Aluminium), operating the Fort William aluminium smelter, were also growing concerned at the costs and reliability of their thrice-weekly ingot train.

Early 2001 saw EWS pull the plug on the daily 'Enterprise' working between Mossend and Fort William, when Arjo Wiggins went over to road haulage only. In June of that year, Freightliner's aluminium ingot traffic went the same way. Furthermore, the Oban line became freight-less too around the same time, when EWS abandoned timber-loading operations at Taynuilt. To summarise this miserable turn of events, the West Highland lines were now left with only two freight trains in each direction per day.

There were one or two rather extraordinary events that would lift the doom and gloom of 2001 in the West Highlands however. The Mallaig Extension was about to appear in Hollywood courtesy of the *Harry Potter* series of movies, with some steam train sequences filmed over the line using GWR 'Hall' class 4-6-0 No 5972 *Olton Hall*. Three days from 31 August–2 September that year saw the unusual visitor, in its special red livery and named *Hogwarts Castle*, make a number of runs over Glenfinnan Viaduct, where the filming was shot from a helicopter. One hundred children from Lochaber High School in Fort William were used as extras for the film *Harry Potter and the Chamber of Secrets*, travelling on the train, with the small village of Glenfinnan becoming a massive hive of activity.

Despite the Great Western locomotive being cleared for running over the whole line between Glasgow and Mallaig, the first run to Glenfinnan on 30 August saw her collide with the edge of the curved platform at Banavie station, her cylinders proving to be too wide for adequate clearance. But No 5972 did manage to get past after the timber-built platform edges were temporarily removed.

On Tuesday 2 October, history was made on the Mallaig line when some of ScotRail's service trains that day were *steam*-hauled. To celebrate the centenary year of the Extension, K1 No 62005 and B1 No 61264 hauled four-coach rakes of Mark 1 coaches on the afternoon and evening workings to/from Mallaig, plus a few extras laid on to give a full day of steam haulage. Originally it was planned to use steam on *all* of that day's Sprinter workings but this wasn't allowed, as journey times had to be extended and there was the possibility of passengers missing booked ferry connections at Mallaig, though ScotRail also provided buses for this purpose.

On the evening of 2 July 2003, 66096 pauses for a fresh token at Bridge of Orchy, leading 37411 *The Scottish Railway Preservation Society* on the 6E16 1758 Fort William–North Blyth empty alumina tankers. Class 66+37 combinations were not particularly unusual on this working, as it was a convenient way of transporting a '37' dead in transit back to Mossend Yard. (David Webster)

The steam-hauled day (nicknamed 'Plandampf': a concept originating in Germany, meaning 'scheduled steam') was a huge success, despite torrential rain, and trains were reportedly full to the point that they became standing room only. Ordinary ScotRail ticket prices were charged too, with a cheap day return from Fort William–Mallaig costing only £7.50. The highlight of the day was arguably when the 1608 Mallaig–Fort William ScotRail service, headed by No 61264, passed No 62005 on the 1627 ex-Fort William at Glenfinnan – both of them running boiler-first. The Plandampf day, which was organised by Highland Railway Heritage, also marked the first time in Britain since 1968 that a timetabled passenger train was steam-hauled.

Filming for *Harry Potter and the Prisoner of Azkaban* brought No 5972 *Olton Hall* back to the Mallaig Extension for seventeen days in early 2003, but not without incident. On 26 February, the locomotive was blamed for starting a massive hillside fire near Glenfinnan Viaduct, after a period of very dry weather. Four fire engines and twenty firefighters were called to the scene, before a helicopter arrived to water-bomb the burning heather. After further filming around Loch Eilt, *Olton Hall* returned to her Carnforth depot home on 6 March, though she would return again for further film sequences over the next few years. High risk of fire was often a reason given by BR/Railtrack/Network Rail over the years when they cancelled steam-hauled trains.

Tourism in the West Highlands was promoted with the 2002 creation of Loch Lomond & The Trossachs National Park, which takes in the southern part of the West Highland Line between Arrochar and Tyndrum. The 96-mile-long West Highland Way had become a very popular attraction by this period, being first established in 1980 along a trail which hugs the side of the railway for most of the route. Many former railway buildings were converted for use by walkers, such as the Bridge of Orchy station building, which was reopened, immaculately preserved in its original condition as a bunkhouse in 2002.

Freight traffic fluctuated somewhat after 2001. The BP oil terminal at Fort William reopened in 2003 for the first time in many a year, with tankers added to the daily alumina train. However, the decline of the Corpach paper mill was complete when the entire plant closed down in September 2005. This was followed over a year later in December 2006 by EWS's decision to dispense with its West Highland timber traffic, with the roads once again being a preferred method of transport. All of this did not look good, given that it was the mill and the associated log trains which had effectively saved the lines from closure four decades previously.

On the other hand, the railway was by now clearly in a much stronger position than it had been then, thanks to the increased tourism and a change in government policy towards railways, helped by Devolution. Under the Scottish Executive, railways were now recognised more for their social and environmental benefits rather than whether or not they made a profit. As a result, several previously closed routes across the country were reopened, while ScotRail continued to receive the large subsidies necessary to run rural routes like the West Highland. October 2004 saw the First Group acquire the new ScotRail franchise, running for the first few years as First ScotRail, before being rebranded simply ScotRail once again in September 2008.

While the timber trains came and went again later in the decade, the oil traffic proved not to be just a flash in the pan and continued to operate to Fort William, eventually as part of a separate train. On the passenger side, some ScotRail trains started to run as separate services from Glasgow to Oban and Mallaig respectively during summer months, to allow for longer train lengths, indicating that passenger loadings were very healthy. But while the scenic views from the train

Showing just how well-used Tyndrum Lower station can be during the summer months, 156478 calls at its single platform on 25 May 2013. An old line-side gradient post can be seen in the foreground, while it is also possible to see where the former Down platform and loop used to be situated. (Author)

were still the top attraction, they had become somewhat restricted along certain stretches of line thanks to the increasing amount of line-side vegetation through the years. In particular, passengers over the Helensburgh–Crianlarich section now had rather interrupted views of the lochs and mountains.

It was clear that the tree issue needed to be addressed if the West Highland lines were to retain their scenic appeal. Thanks to years of campaigning by the Friends of the West Highland Lines, Network Rail agreed to a special tree-felling programme co-ordinated with the help of the group and other organisations such as Loch Lomond & The Trossachs National Park, to restore some of the lost scenic views. 2010 saw work take place over a 350-metre stretch immediately south of Arrochar & Tarbet station, where the line goes over the A83 road and crosses an embankment, opening up magnificent views of the 'Arrochar Alps'. A further £23,000 grant saw clearing take place at several spots the following year, such as the heavily wooded area around Glen Falloch Viaduct, Loch Awe and to the north of Crianlarich. Work between 2012–13 saw the area around Glenfinnan Viaduct tackled, with more scheduled for years to come at a variety of locations. This project has been a huge success story for the Friends of the West Highland Lines, who were instrumental in ensuring the survival and promotion of the railway through the years.

Extreme weather conditions in recent times have wreaked havoc on the West Highland lines on a few occasions, just as they have everywhere else. Heavy snow in late February 2010 was followed by avalanches on the mountains between Tyndrum and Bridge of Orchy, blocking the line for over a week. At each of the four affected sites there was estimated to be around 5,000m^3 of snow.

Heavy summer rainfall was responsible for the landslide which caused another accident in the Pass of Brander on 6 June 2010, in which eight passengers were injured. Two-car Sprinter 156499 was working the 1820 Glasgow–Oban service when fallen rocks caused it to derail, with the leading vehicle left hanging precariously over the embankment just above the A85 road around the edge of Loch Awe. A minor fire underneath the leading car was also reported. However, the quick reactions of the train crew helped to ensure that any major disaster was averted and that all passengers were quickly evacuated from the stricken DMU. It was notable that the guard that day was also involved in the 1997 derailment, which occurred at almost the same spot near Falls of Cruachan station.

The recovery of the derailed Class 156 was a complex affair, due to the lack of space afforded by the steep embankment and the road running on a narrow ledge next to the loch. After stabilising the leading vehicle of the unit, a road-mounted crane was used to hoist it to safety on 11 June. The rear vehicle was able to be removed by rail the same day, being hauled away by West Coast Railways' 37676. After an investigation it was found that the fallen boulders had been dislodged by soil erosion and had once again slipped underneath the wire screen connected to the stone signals. As a result, the semaphores were not activated to give warning of the danger ahead.

More torrential rain two years later, on 28 June 2012, was responsible for the derailment on the shores of Loch Treig, involving GBRf's 66734 *The Eco Express*, which was hauling the 0635 North Blyth–Fort William, loaded alumina tankers. The locomotive hit a large boulder pushed on to the track by a landslide and crashed down an embankment to rest between the trees only metres away from the loch side. Five of the twenty-four wagons were also derailed. The driver, shaken but uninjured, was airlifted to Fort William. There was another landslide that same day which closed the line near Arrochar.

A miserable day at Upper Tyndrum on 26 June 2012 sees a four-car Sprinter set of 156476/474 pause with the 1605 Mallaig–Glasgow. Heavy rain was continuous throughout the rest of that particular week and two days later caused the landslide that derailed Class 66 No 66734 at Loch Treig. (Author)

As at the Pass of Brander, accessibility was a problem when it came to clearing up the scene of the Loch Treig accident, with no public roads leading to that particular stretch of line. It was decided that, due to the difficulty involved to remove it, it would be better to leave the derailed Class 66 where it stood for the time being, while the authorities explored various options of what to do. Meanwhile, some of the re-railed wagons were stabled temporarily at Corrour station siding. This caused great concern to the new owners of the remote station restaurant there, with the tankers supposedly obscuring the view out of the window.

Eventually it was decided that the most practical and cost-effective solution regarding the derailed 66734 was to write off the locomotive and scrap it

No 156478 leaves Falls of Cruachan on 25 May 2013 with the Summer Saturdays 1037 Glasgow–Oban. The waiting shelter is a recent addition while the floral displays add character to the halt – a tradition started by the late Brian Bentham, a local volunteer who took care of the station's upkeep. HITRANS gave Falls of Cruachan the award of 'Most Improved Local Station 2011'. (Author)

on site. This finally took place in autumn 2013, after a special roadway had to be constructed to allow access for workers.

Another accident occurred in the Pass of Brander on 18 July 2012, once again near to the site of the previous incidents. The 1256 Oban–Glasgow service hit a small landslide one mile east of Falls of Cruachan, though this time the train did not derail, with the crew and all sixty-six passengers avoiding injury. The service was made up of four-car Sprinter set 156478/453 and the rear unit was able to transport the passengers back to Oban after examination. It is believed that this landslide was caused by a blocked culvert, with the fallen rocks and soil able to once again reach the track without tripping the 'Anderson's Piano' system (see chapter one).

It must be remembered that the weather conditions during the summer of 2012 were rather exceptional. Snow problems in the West Highlands have also generally been fewer since the 1980s, when Eastfield depot's independent snowploughs were kept very busy during winter. There were even suggestions in recent years that the Cruach snow shed on Rannoch Moor could be removed, since it had fallen into disrepair.

All in all, the privatisation era has had mixed fortunes for freight on the West Highland lines, with an increase in traffic at the beginning turning into a major downturn, mostly on account of the economy. However, passenger levels have increased dramatically, as attested to by ScotRail running extra or longer trains in recent years. The summer of 2014 will see the number of services between Glasgow and Oban doubled, to six a day in each direction, while the 'Jacobite' steam service has started to operate two separate trains on certain days due to popular demand. This heartening increase in popularity of the lines can be put down to several factors. Good marketing, such as the emphasis on the *Harry Potter* connection, has been the main one, with other factors such as increasing petrol prices and higher popularity of outdoor activities also contributing. But as ever, most of these factors come down to the scenic splendour along the routes; something which will never change in the face of modernisation.

5

Traction

Class 20

The English Electric Class 20s were once a familiar sight on West Highland metals, proving their worth both for shunting duties and frontline freight work. One of the first diesel classes to appear in the area, they supplemented both the Class 27 and 37 fleets before largely disappearing in the 1990s.

20181 is pictured stabled in the Down sidings at Crianlarich station on 14 February 1987. This locomotive had a working life of just twenty years, being withdrawn in November of that year, though several of its classmates have survived in mainline service into the twenty-first century. (David Webster)

Factfile

Power type:	Diesel-electric
Builder:	English Electric (Vulcan Foundry, Newton-le-Willows and Robert Stephenson & Hawthorns, Darlington)
Build date:	1957–68
Total produced:	228
Wheel configuration:	Bo-Bo
Engine:	English Electric 8SVT Mk. 2
Weight:	73 tonnes
Maximum tractive effort:	42,000lb
Brake force:	35 tonnes
Max speed:	60/75mph
Route availability:	RA5
Nickname(s):	Choppers

Sub-classes Used on West Highland lines
20/0

(20001–228)   Original, as-built locomotives

20/3

(20301–315)   Refurbished with modified cab layout and extra fuel tanks

20/9

(20901–906)   Modified for use by Hunslet-Barclay on weedkiller trains

Early Years

The Class 20s were originally conceived as English Electric Type 1 locomotives, with their single cab design betraying their status as one of the earlier types introduced as part of the 1955 British Rail Modernisation Plan. They were intended purely for freight use, with the first twenty 'pilot scheme' locomotives delivered in 1957–58, and a further 208 examples rolled out between 1959 and 1968.

From 1961, the 20s began appearing on the West Highland lines, mostly working in pairs coupled nose-to-nose due to their single cab layout and relatively low horsepower. Whilst used mostly on freight workings, they were trialled on passenger services on both the Fort William and Mallaig roads too. They became more well established in the area after the end of steam in 1962, by then used almost exclusively for freight. And the opening of the Corpach pulp and paper mill in 1964 saw 20s start to appear on the associated timber traffic.

Eastfield depot was responsible for the maintenance of the 20s through most of the period they ran in the West Highlands. The first machines allocated here in the 1960s had the earlier front end design, with folding headcode discs used to signify what type of train they were hauling. Some locomotives had three-piece miniature snowploughs fitted and all had cab-side recesses for tablet-catching apparatus, though only the former would prove to be of much use in the West Highlands. They also had sliding cab windows to aid tablet exchanges.

1970–80s

The 1970s saw the 20s in regular use on West Highland goods traffic, working both singly and in pairs. They carried the same 'blue star' multiple-working equipment as the Class 27s working over the line, meaning that 20+27 doubleheaders could also be seen on occasions. The light weight of this class made them especially ideal for engineers' trains or any pick-up freights.

Since the end of the steam era, the Class 20s, like all other main line diesels, had the 'D' prefix dropped from their original numbers. Thus the pioneer of the fleet, D8000, became 8000 and so forth. The TOPS renumbering scheme in 1973 saw all locomotives officially become Class 20s, when all were renumbered in sequence with the '20' prefix (e.g. 8001 became 20001). The exceptions were 8000 (becoming 20050), 8050 (20128) and 8128 (20228). Later in the 1970s, the use of front end headcode discs was abolished and eventually many of the class would have their discs removed.

During that decade, the withdrawal of some of the less successful diesel types, such as the Class 17s and 29s, resulted in many English-based Class 20s being cascaded north to Scotland, with many going to Eastfield. Many were part of the later build batch constructed between 1966 and 1968, which carried four-character headcode panels at each end in place of the discs. These panels also became redundant in the late 1970s, with the four-character display replaced by two white marker lights, known as a 'domino' pattern. The original Scottish batch of locomotives also had their tablet-catching recesses plated over.

The Class 20s became more prominent on the West Highland lines in the 1980s after the introduction of Class 37s on passenger trains. All locomotives had their through steam-heating pipes removed but Eastfield's 20045/85 actually had them refitted in 1983 for double-heading with Class 37s on Glasgow–Oban/Fort William trains. By this time Class 20s were nearly always seen working in pairs throughout the BR network, but the West Highlands became one of the few places they could be seen working solo – and nose-first! There was normally a 20 used as the Fort William yard pilot throughout the 1980s, so it was inevitable that it would be called into passenger action on occasions. The late afternoon Fort William–Mallaig service, sometimes operating as a 'mixed' train, became an occasional turn. More usual work for the local 20 would be trip workings to the aluminium smelter and Corpach mill.

The introduction of RETB signalling to the West Highland routes in 1987 resulted in three Class 20s – 20114/27/38 – being fitted with the necessary equipment, which included large aerials mounted on their nose ends. They also carried snowploughs and 20127 featured a high-intensity headlight on its cab end. From this point onwards, only the aforementioned three could operate north of Helensburgh.

It was 20138 which once had to be called upon to work a passenger train to Glasgow – managing to haul the 1415 ex-Fort William all alone and nose-first as far as Crianlarich where a Class 37 took over, on 13 May 1988. On 28 May, the other two RETB-fitted machines, 20114/127, made a rare appearance for the class on an SRPS railtour, double-heading the Gourock–Mallaig train between Dumbarton–Fort William–Gourock.

Sadly, the replacement of loco-hauled trains on the Glasgow-Oban/Fort William/Mallaig circuit shortly after coincided with the three RETB-fitted 'Choppers' being reallocated to other work, and shunting duties at Fort William once again became the preserve of Class 08s.

Decline

By the early 1990s, Class 20s were virtually extinct from the West Highlands, save for a very occasional appearance by a pair of locomotives from the Hunslet-Barclay '20/9' fleet top-and-tailing weedkiller trains during the summer months. The company employed six of the class, refurbished and renumbered as 20901–906 at the private company's Kilmarnock headquarters. Each locomotive was named after one of the group's employees and they saw service all over the UK throughout the 1990s, before being sold to Direct Rail Services (DRS) after privatisation.

Since Hunslet-Barclay lost the weedkilling contract, there has been barely a trace of Class 20 power on the West Highland lines to date, which is a reflection on the type's overall reduction in use more than anything else. The 1990s saw the entire fleet downsized rapidly, and by the turn of the new millennium only a handful remained in service – mostly with Carlisle-based DRS. Most were refurbished as '20/3s'. One of these machines – 20302 – made a glorious return to the West Highlands between 17–18 July 2009, being paired with 37069 on Spitfire Railtours' 'West Highlander' from Preston to Oban, Fort William and Mallaig. Better still, on 28 September 2013, 20308/309 made a surprise appearance double-heading a Pathfinder charter from Glasgow to Fort William.

Liveries

From new, all Class 20s carried BR standard Brunswick green livery. This was the condition in which they were first seen on the West Highland lines, before many received small yellow warning panels at each end. Eventually the yellow ends were extended to cover the whole 'face' of the locomotives, but with BR's 'corporate blue' colour scheme also spreading to the class. Full yellow panels were by now a requirement and eventually all members of the class, bar 20014, received the new livery, complete with BR 'double arrow' symbols.

Eastfield TMD's (Traction Maintenance Depot) adoption of the 'Scottie Dog' depot motif spread to the class from the early 1980s, printed on the body-sides. Unlike on the class 37s, it was always small in size. The three RETB-fitted machines – 20114/27/38 – all received this embellishment. While 20114/127 carried BR blue colours, 20138 received what came to be known as 'Railfreight red stripe' livery during the mid 1980s, with full-height 'double arrow' logos, red solebars and wrap-around yellow ends over the cab-sides with black window surrounds.

The Hunslet-Barclay '20/9s' were painted in a two-tone grey livery with red solebars. DRS locomotives have always carried an overall dark blue livery, both an original and revised style, with red buffer beams being a distinctive feature.

Class 21 and 29

While most diesel classes associated with the West Highland lines have been undoubted success stories, the same cannot be said of the Glasgow-built North British Type 2s. Latterly categorised as Class 21 and 29, the locomotives were built as part of the 1955 British Railways Modernisation Plan, but only survived in traffic for a mere decade before being withdrawn.

D6130 was one of the North British Type 2s re-engined with a Paxman power unit and classified as Class 29. It is seen leaving the West Highland main line at Craigendoran Junction in August 1968 at the head of an Oban–Glasgow service. Note the overhead wires of the North Clyde electric line from Helensburgh Central joining in the foreground. (Allan Trotter, Eastbank Model Railway Club)

Factfile

Power type:	Diesel-electric
Builder:	North British Locomotive Co.
Build date:	1958–60
Total produced:	58 (20 rebuilt as Class 29)
Wheel configuration:	Bo-Bo
Engine:	MAN L12V18/21 (re-engined Paxman Ventura)
Weight:	73 tonnes
Maximum tractive effort:	45,001lb (Class 29: 47,001lb)
Brake force:	42 tonnes
Max speed:	75/80mph
Route availability:	RA5

Story of the NBLs

Between 1958 and 1959, the North British Locomotive Company, based in Springburn, Glasgow, built ten of their own Type 2 Bo-Bo diesel electric locomotives. They were intended for evaluation by BR, who were experimenting with different types of newly-built diesel locomotives at the time before coming up with a definite game plan to oust steam traction from the national network. But before they had even entered service, BR made the bizarre decision to press ahead and order another forty-eight of the same locomotives.

The North British Type 2s were not initially intended for working on the West Highland lines; they were instead allocated to depots in London, Ipswich and Aberdeen. However, right from the outset the locomotives were plagued by continual engine failures. Those based south of the border were in fact so lamented by the English crews that they were sent back to Scotland in 1960. The following year, the class (numbered D6100-6157) began use on Glasgow–Oban services via Callander – normally double-headed as insurance against failures.

The locomotives started to appear on the Glasgow–Fort William/Mallaig circuit when steam was ending in 1962, working alongside Class 27s. However, their appalling reliability record eventually led to many locomotives being re-engined – their German-built MAN power units being replaced by Paxman equivalents. Twenty of the class were so treated between 1965 and 1967 – these were D6100-3/6-8/12-4/6/9/21/3/4/9/30/2/3/7. The new engines brought a significant improvement – so much so that the locomotives were now allowed to work passenger trains singly as opposed to double-headed! The re-engined examples also received four-character backlit headcode boxes at each end, replacing the headcode discs originally carried by the class. They also had their front-end gangway doors sealed shut as a result. In addition, it was at around this time that the BR TOPS system had all of the NBL diesels listed as either Class 21 or 29, though they would never survive long enough to be officially renumbered. The as-built locomotives were classified as 21s while the re-engined examples were 29s.

After a brief stint on the West Highland lines in the early 1960s, the troublesome NBLs were largely dropped in favour of Class 27s. However, the Paxman-built 29s started to become established from 1967, working solo on passenger trains. Freight workings were rarer and the class were never paired with 27s, which had different multiple-working equipment. The remaining MAN-engined 21s were already being consigned to the scrapyard around this time, withdrawn after only seven years in traffic! By August 1968 all were gone, leaving only the twenty Class 29s.

But even the re-engining programme was not enough to save the 29s, which were still not particularly solid performers. BR took the view that they were a small, non-standard class, along with some of the other unsuccessful diesel types such as Class 17s, and decided to cut their losses. Most locomotives would survive in traffic until 1971, with the West Highlands still one of their main stamping grounds until the very end. Most were scrapped shortly after, with none being preserved. All in all, the story of these locomotives was one sorry episode for BR; even more incredible when one considers that the locomotives they replaced on the West Highland lines – the Stanier Class 5s – had a lifespan totalling over three decades.

Liveries

All NBL Type 2s originally carried BR Brunswick green livery, with no lining. This was enhanced by some locomotives receiving half-yellow warning panels from 1962 onwards.

Locomotives rebuilt with Paxman engines received a new style of BR two-tone green livery: light and dark shades separated by a thin white body-side stripe. All carried new square-shaped yellow panels around their headcode boxes.

Eight of the Class 29s – D6100/7-9/19/24/9/37 – received BR 'corporate blue' livery with full yellow ends. One of the Class 21s, D6109, was also painted blue, after it had received many of the Class 29 modifications such as new headcode boxes.

Class 27

The introduction of BRCW Class 27 locomotives in 1961 marked a watershed moment in West Highland railway history: the changeover from steam to diesel traction. The class would go on to dominate passenger and freight traffic for nearly two decades, before they were phased out in favour of the more powerful Class 37s.

27043 prepares to couple up to a Glasgow-bound train at Oban in April 1977. As can be seen, semaphore signals were still extant at the terminus during this period, as well as the original platforms and station building hidden behind the train. (Allan Trotter, Eastbank Model Railway Club)

Factfile

Power type:	Diesel-electric
Builder:	Birmingham Railway Carriage and Wagon Co. (Smethwick, Birmingham)
Build date:	1961–62
Total produced:	69
Wheel configuration:	Bo-Bo
Engine:	Sulzer 6LDA28B
Weight:	74–77 tonnes
Maximum tractive effort:	40,000lb
Brake force:	35 tonnes
Max speed:	90mph
Route availability:	RA5

Sub-classes Used on West Highland lines

27/0

(27001–044)   As-built condition, either with or without steam heat boilers

27/1

(27101–124)   Fitted with push-pull equipment

27/2

(27201–212)   Fitted with Electric Train Heat (ETH) generators

Story of the 27s

The Class 27s, together with the earlier built 26s, were originally classified by BR as BRCW Type 2s. The 27s were a development of the 26s, with a similar design but greater horsepower. The only obvious difference was that the 27s carried roof-mounted four-digit headcode boxes at each end, as opposed to the discs seen on 26s.

There was a sign of things to come on the West Highland lines when the first twenty-three Class 27s – D5347–5369 – were delivered brand new to Glasgow's Eastfield depot between 1961 and 1962. The other forty-six members of the class would be allocated to the Midland and North Eastern regions of BR. The year of 1962 saw the locomotives gradually introduced into traffic on both the Glasgow Queen Street–Fort William–Mallaig and Glasgow Buchanan Street–Oban routes. After an interim period operating beside their predecessors, by late 1962 the BRCW Type 2s had taken over all freight and passenger workings from the remaining K1 and 'Black Five' steam locomotives. The type also established themselves on the Connel Ferry–Ballachulish branch line.

The locomotives then dominated West Highland passenger traffic, but with the NBL Type 2s (Class 21s and 29s) also helping out. The 27s were frequently double-headed too on the heavier workings and all were fitted with boilers to provide steam heating to the carriages during the colder months of the year. Many also carried three-piece miniature snowploughs at both ends; the idea had been to remove these during the summer months, but many locomotives ended up carrying them all year round. The Eastfield allocation also had T-shaped cab-side recesses to allow tablet catchers to be fitted, even though these were not used in the West Highlands. They also had the sliding cab windows seen on the Class 20s, unlike the English-based 27s, which had droplight windows.

The late 1960s saw the newly re-engined North British Bo-Bos start to establish more of a foothold on passenger work to Oban/Fort William/Mallaig for a few years until their withdrawal, which allowed the 27s to assume full control. Another main development around this time was BR's decision to concentrate the entire Class 27 fleet in Scotland. As a result, English-based locomotives D5370–5415 were all transferred to Scotland, with some appearing in the West Highlands. The first nine machines, D5370–5378, initially allocated to Thornaby depot, did not carry steam heat boilers and were easily identified by their lack of water tanks between the bogies. These machines started to appear regularly on freight traffic to Fort William and Oban.

The 27s became by far and away the most dominant motive power north of Craigendoran in the 1970s. The adoption of TOPS numbering in 1973 saw two distinctive sub-classes created to separate the twenty-four locomotives fitted with push-pull equipment for Glasgow–Edinburgh services. These became '27/1s' while the un-modified machines became '27/0s'. Shortly after, twelve locomotives were fitted with Electric Train Heat (ETH) generators for the same workings. These became '27/2s' and were all converted from existing 27/1s. Both 27/1s and 27/2s were dedicated to the Edinburgh–Glasgow shuttles, but they also regularly worked in the West Highlands, supplementing the more usual 27/0s. Most 27/1s and 27/2s did not carry snowploughs.

The most memorable duties for 27s on the West Highland routes during this period were the London Euston sleeper and the heavy timber trains which ran between Crianlarich and Corpach pulp mill. But by the end of the 1970s, their reliability was starting to deteriorate, with engine-room fires a notorious problem. The more powerful Class 37s were seen as a better alternative and the mass transfer of many of these machines to Scotland in early 1981 spelt the end for 27s in the West Highlands. By the following year, the English Electric machines had largely displaced them, as withdrawals of the 27s started to gather pace across the country. Push-pull and ETH equipment was removed from the remaining 27/1s and 27/2s, which were all renumbered as 27045–066.

The class still occasionally deputised for Class 37s on Glasgow–Oban/Fort William services into the 1980s, as well as on some of the freight workings. But by 1986/87, the few remaining members of the class in traffic were relegated to light goods turns, especially engineers' traffic. After making their final appearances on the Glasgow–Fort William route in the summer of 1987, August saw the very last member of the class, 27008, withdrawn from traffic. Luckily eight of them would survive into preservation, including 27001/005, owned by the SRPS at Bo'ness.

Liveries

Initially, all 27s carried BR Brunswick green livery, with bold white body-side stripes and window surrounds as seen on Class 26s. These were either with or without half-yellow warning panels, though the mid 1960s would see all members of the class receive them. By this time, full yellow ends became mandatory on all diesels and some received them whilst still in green livery.

Shortly after, locomotives started to receive the new BR 'corporate blue' colours with full yellow ends, all of the class eventually being so treated. However, D5370 still carried BR green into 1974 – even after receiving TOPS numbers to become 27024! The yellow ends on the blue machines extended around the cab-side windows in common with many other types of diesels. Sadly, the 27s were not around long enough to receive any other liveries in their lifetime and even the last ones withdrawn in 1987 were in roughly the same condition. The only notable alterations made were the changes from D-prefix to TOPS numbers, followed soon after by 'domino' headcode box displays replacing the four-character codes. In addition, many locomotives still in traffic in the 1980s received the Inverness 'Highland Stag' and Eastfield 'Scottie Dog' depot motifs. The 'Scottie Dogs' were of the small size, printed on the body-sides.

Class 37

For many years, the 1960s-built English Electric Class 37s were the dominant traction on the lines west of Craigendoran. Still at work over three decades after their introduction in the area, the '37s' really are the quintessential West Highland diesel locomotives.

Factfile

Power type:	Diesel-electric
Builder:	English Electric (Vulcan Foundry, Newton-le-Willows and Robert Stephenson & Hawthorns, Darlington)
Build date:	1960–65
Total produced:	309
Wheel configuration:	Co-Co
Engine:	English Electric 12CSVT
Weight:	102–107 tonnes
Maximum tractive effort:	55,500lb
Brake force:	50 tonnes
Max speed:	80/90mph
Route availability:	RA5, RA7 (Class 37/7 only)
Nickname(s):	Tractors, Growlers, Syphons

It is 7.05 a.m. on 15 July 2002 as special EWS claret-liveried 37401 *The Royal Scotsman* pauses at Arrochar & Tarbet with the 0450 Edinburgh–Fort William portion of the 'Caledonian Sleeper'. This '37/4' was always kept in superb external condition by Motherwell depot staff for hauling its namesake luxury touring train. (Author)

Sub-classes Used on West Highland lines

37/0
(37001-308)	Original, un-modified condition, either with steam heat boiler or without.

37/4
(37401-431)	Refurbished with Electric Train Heating (nowadays known as Electric Train Supply or ETS).

37/5
(37501-521, 37667-699)	Refurbished for freight use – no train heat.

37/6
(37601-612)	'37/5s' modified for use on Eurostar 'Nightstar' services. Through ETS wiring but no generator.

37/7
(37701-719, 37796-803, 37883-899)	Refurbished for freight use with extra ballast weight added. No train heat.

Early Years

Introduced in the early 1960s as part of the British Rail Modernisation Plan, the Class 37s were originally classified as English Electric Type 3s. Their construction was split between the Vulcan Foundry at Newton-le-Willows and Robert Stephenson & Hawthorns of Darlington. Designed for both freight and passenger use, Eastfield depot first received an allocation of the class during the 1960s – all freight-only machines built without train heating boilers. They were trialled for a week working goods traffic as far as Corpach paper mill, though the local engineers' teams reported an increased amount of track wear, so their use was discontinued. Renumbered under the new BR TOPS scheme as Class 37, the locomotives were not used again in the West Highlands until January 1978, when boiler-fitted 37108/111 were added to Eastfield's allocation of the class. Many of them were tested on both passenger and freight workings to Oban, Fort William and Mallaig.

The Class 37s were not used extensively in Scotland until the early 1980s. Primarily based south of the border, a number of the class were gradually cascaded to Scotland to replace Type 2 traction (Class 25, 26 and 27) in the Highlands. Following some success with the second round of trials, between 1980–82 Eastfield depot received further members of the class, which gradually took over from Class 27s on all passenger and freight turns to Oban, Fort William and Mallaig. The initial allocation was made up of 37011/2/4/21/2/5-7/33/5/7/9/43/51/81/5/108/11/2/4. All were dual-braked, with the exception of 37011/25/35/114 which had vacuum brakes only, precluding them from hauling Mark 2 coaches or air-braked freights. The majority of locomotives were drafted in from BR's Eastern Region, transferred from depots such as March and Stratford.

They offered increased power, with a higher tractive effort and improved reliability compared to the life-expired Class 27s. However, it soon became apparent that the tight curves on the West Highland lines were taking their toll on the big locomotives' wheels, with excess tyre wear and noise a frequent problem. (The screeching sound produced from the wheels earned them the nickname 'The Banshees' from drivers.) Various experiments were tried to correct this: 37175 was fitted with self-steering CP5 bogies and thinner traction tyres; 37112/192 received 'graphite sticks' mounted to their bogies; 37081 was given 'Lausanne'-type flange greasers as used on Class 303 EMUs. The latter modification was the most successful and was later adopted on other members of the class.

Eastfield's early Class 37 allocation included a dedicated pool of locomotives fitted with steam heat boilers for use on passenger trains. The rest of the allocation – all 'no heat' examples – were used purely for freight work. All of these original, un-refurbished locomotives, became known as the '37/0' sub-class, which included both 'Phase 1' and 'Phase 2' locomotives. The 'Phase 1' type had split headcode boxes (by then plated over) and gangway doors at each end. This contrasted with the 'Phase 2' examples which had centre-fitted headcode panels and roof-mounted air horns. In addition, many of the Eastfield 37s also carried three-piece miniature snowploughs for working over the West Highland lines. Unlike the Class 27s, the 37s usually carried these all year round.

As the last Class 27s were gradually ousted from the Oban/Fort William/ Mallaig routes, their replacements settled into traffic and were soon adopted with the first of many personalisations that would closely identify them with the West Highlands. 37012/26/27/43/81 were all named after nearby lochs – *Loch Rannoch, Loch Awe, Loch Eil, Loch Lomond* and *Loch Long*. It was also around this time that Eastfield's famous 'Scottie Dog' depot motif first appeared on the body-sides of many locomotives.

The 1980s saw BR gradually eliminate steam heating from passenger trains as more Mark 2 and Mark 3 coaching stock was brought into use. From 1983–85, the daily Fort William–London Euston sleeper had a 37 hauling an ETHEL unit within the train as the 37/0s did not have the required Electric Train Heating (ETH) for hauling the Mark 3s. A more efficient solution was implemented when, in 1985, thirty-one Class 37s were refurbished with ETH generators replacing their steam heat boilers. Eastfield received seventeen members of the new '37/4' sub-class with the remainder going to Inverness and Cardiff Canton depots. The most obvious new detail features were plated-over centre-headcode panels with new marker lights, high-intensity headlights and ETH jumper cables on each nose end. All were painted in the striking new BR 'Large Logo' livery, complete with three-piece miniature snowploughs.

From October 1985, Eastfield's seventeen 37/4s started to take over all West Highland passenger work from 37/0s, which were relegated to freight duties

On a wet 3 August 1985, 37111 *Loch Eil Outward Bound* has an 'ETHEL' unit for company on the 0550 Glasgow–Fort William (with through sleeping cars from London Euston), seen arriving at Tulloch to cross the 0840 Fort William–Glasgow. Semaphore signals were still in abundance at this time, though steam-heated carriages were on the way out. (David Webster)

and gradually reallocated elsewhere. The introduction of RETB signalling to the routes between 1987 and 88 saw all of the 37/4s and remaining 37/0s fitted with the necessary radios and cab display units (CDUs) – the bonnet-mounted aerials at each end being a telltale sign of this. From this point onwards, only those locomotives fitted with RETB would be able to operate, meaning that for a long time, freight and passenger traffic would be almost exclusively hauled by 37401-413 and 37422-425. Most of these were gradually named (see table on page 90).

After almost eight years of Class 37 heaven for rail photographers in the West Highlands, their monopoly on passenger and freight traffic came to an abrupt end on 23 January 1989, when Class 156 'Super Sprinter' DMUs took over all passenger services with the exception of the Euston sleeper. Eastfield retained the majority of the 37/4 fleet for freight, charter and sleeper haulage, but the sub-class also started to spread their wings elsewhere in the country. Most were soon repainted into the smart InterCity 'Mainline' livery to match the sleeper stock, which became their prime duty into the 1990s.

The years 1991–92 saw Welsh-based 37/4s 37428/430 transferred to Eastfield and both were to become regulars over the West Highland lines throughout the decade. They were transferred to Motherwell TMD along with the rest of the fleet after the closure of Eastfield in November 1992, but the duties of the class remained the same. This included, would you believe it, daytime passenger haulage to Oban, Fort William and Mallaig, which was reintroduced for the summer season only in 1992. These 'Young Explorer' trains continued for the summer timetables in 1993–94 to Oban and Fort William only, mainly employing 37/4s. A number of 37/0s also saw use, with train heating not normally being required at that time of year.

While daytime passenger haulage finished for the class again after 1994, there was still a decent amount of freight traffic around. Newly-created freight company TransRail took over operations after acquiring the Class 37s allocated to the West Highland routes. In 1996, TransRail was taken over by the English Welsh & Scottish Railway (EWS), who took their time in repainting many of the locomotives. As a result, the the mid to late 1990s was one of the most interesting periods for 37 followers, with all kinds of colourful liveries in evidence.

The 37/0 sub-class started to be seen more regularly on freight traffic again in the 1990s, appearing along with the refurbished 37/5s. From 1998, Eurostar's 37/6s even became regulars, when Freightliner began hiring the locomotives to handle the aluminium ingot traffic between Fort William and Coatbridge. All of the locomotives in this sub-class had been refurbished with flush front ends and were used on this particular circuit because Freightliner had no Class 37s of their

---

CLASS 37/4S BASED AT EASTFIELD TMD

1986-89

37401	Mary Queen of Scots
37402	Oor Wullie
37403	Isle of Mull*
37404	Ben Cruachan
37405	Strathclyde Region
37406	The Saltire Society
37407	Loch Long
37408	Loch Rannoch
37409	Loch Awe
37410	Aluminium 100
37411	The Institution of Railway Signal Engineers
37412	Loch Lomond
37413	Loch Eil Outward Bound
37422	Unnamed
37423	Sir Murray Morrison 1873-1948 Pioneer of the British Aluminium Industry
37424	Glendarroch*
37425	Sir Robert McAlpine/Concrete Bob

*37403 and 424 latterly swapped names

own, or any equivalent types with a suitable route availability for working over the West Highland.

As the new millennium arrived, so too did new traction for EWS, who were by then the dominant freight operator in the West Highlands. The General Motors Class 66s had already taken over a large amount of traffic from the 37s since their arrival on the British railway scene in 1998. Route availability issues had so far kept the 66s away from the West Highland lines, but their eventual approval for use between Craigendoran–Fort William came in September 2000. They took over all freight workings from the 37s with the exception of the aluminium ingots and timber workings to Taynuilt on the Oban line.

The decline of freight traffic in the West Highlands was clear to see when these remaining Class 37-hauled flows ceased to operate in the summer of 2001. From this point onwards, the class continued to appear on the remaining traffic from time to time, but the only booked 37-hauled trains in the area were the 'Royal Scotsman' luxury train and the ScotRail 'Caledonian Sleeper'. The sleeper continued to utilise the veteran Type 3s despite the adjoining Inverness and Aberdeen portions going over to Class 67 haulage in 2000 and 2001 respectively.

The Scottish-based 37/4 fleet continued to provide the motive power for the sleeper, as they had done since 1985. Between 2001 and 2004 the Motherwell WKBM pool consisted by and large of the same locomotives. These were 37401/5/8/10/1/5/6/8/21/26–8. Various ideas were bounced around regarding their future on the service. There were suggestions of using Class 66s with generator cars but this idea came to nothing. Class 57s were also speculated as possible replacements. Furthermore, there was talk of a large number of 37/4s receiving overhauls and reliability improvements but in the end only 37406/17/22/5 were so treated, mainly for work in South Wales.

Speculation about the introduction of Class 67s on the Fort William sleeper gathered pace from 2003 onwards and it was expected that they could soon replace the 37s at short notice. However, one stay of execution turned into another for the English Electric machines until it was finally confirmed by First ScotRail that 67s would take over from the summer 2006 timetable change. The decision had been long expected and the previous few years had seen enthusiasts from all across the country head to the Highlands to photograph and travel on the sleeper as a result.

The 37s had generally been very reliable during their long tenure hauling the sleeper, though latterly there had been a rising rate of failures – something completely unacceptable for First ScotRail, especially when it happened on the remotest parts of the West Highland main line; although their replacement was not just down to a reliability issue. EWS were rationalising their locomotive fleet and were planning to get rid of the last of their 37s very soon anyway.

The 37/4s' regular sleeper diagram was re-timed slightly in late 2004 but generally remained the same for many years. Latterly it was:

1Y11	0450 Edinburgh–Fort William
1B01	1955 Fort William–Edinburgh (1910 on Sundays)

Sleeper Farewell

For the final few months of Class 37 haulage on 1Y11/1B01 in early 2006, the Motherwell WKBM pool consisted for most of the time of 37401/6/16/7/27. It was most fitting that the very last week (3–9 June) saw the duties shared between two former Eastfield stalwarts: 37401 and 405. The latter locomotive had only just been reallocated to Motherwell depot a matter of weeks before, being reactivated from storage after a couple of years of solid working south of the border. More interesting still was that the diagram alternated between the two different locomotives all week. The normal practice for a number of years was for the same locomotive to take charge of 1Y11/1B01 for four consecutive days before another one took its place. In this case, however, it was arranged for 37401 to haul the train on June 3–4/6/8, while 37405 was in charge on 5 June and 7 June, bringing the curtain down on the very last workings on 9 June.

After twenty-five years of service, the end had finally come for Class 37s on West Highland passenger trains and the 'Caledonian Sleeper' was to become Class 67-hauled from 10 June. For First ScotRail, that was the plan anyway. Unsurprisingly to many, the 37s made an emphatic comeback only weeks later on 29 July, when 37406 *The Saltire Society* stood in for an unavailable Type 5 on the northbound service, returning south on the corresponding working the following day. The next five months would see the 37s continue to make more occasional appearances as problems were ironed out on the 67s. Number 37406 worked the entire diagram for four consecutive days, 4–7 August. On 4 October it was the turn of ex-Inverness 37417 *Richard Trevithick* to work the train in both directions, before hauling the southbound working on 29 October between Glen Douglas and Braidhurst Loop, near Motherwell, after 67009 developed a DSD (Driver Safety Device) fault. No 37417 worked 1B01 the whole way on 15 November. December saw 37406 again power the return working for four solid days, from 8 to 11 December. This time it really was the end for the 37s, some six months after the scheduled changeover. The class has never worked the train since.

Decline

The EWS 37 fleet continued to make sporadic appearances on West Highland freight workings after they had lost their foothold on the sleeper service, well after the Class 66s became established in the area. This went on into 2007, even after EWS had pulled out of the overnight timber traffic and Motherwell depot closed its doors for the final time, with EWS's Scottish locomotives thereafter having to use the minor maintenance facilities at Mossend and at Millerhill in Edinburgh. For the first time since the early 1980s, there was no longer a dedicated fleet of Class 37s based in Scotland for use on the West Highland lines. Despite this, pairs of 37/4s still covered occasionally for 66s on the daily Mossend–Fort William and return 'Enterprise' working. And on the rare occasions that they ran, the MoD workings to Glen Douglas often produced English Electric haulage as well.

While 66s were the booked motive power for freight traffic between Craigendoran and Fort William, the Oban and Mallaig routes remained out of bounds for them due to their high axle load. Therefore there was still a requirement for 37s to be used on any occasional engineers' traffic, specifically ballast trains. For a long time EWS were responsible for such work and this continued after the company's takeover by DB Schenker in 2008. One of the most notable instances was on 27 April 2010, when 37425 *Balchder y Cymoedd/Pride of the Valleys* worked a Mossend–Taynuilt return 'Autoballaster' in its heritage repaint BR 'Large Logo' livery. It reached the Mallaig Extension to work a series of the same trains between Fort William and Arisaig on 1 and 2 June. However, its northbound run from Mossend to Fort William on 31 May saw it fail at Glen Douglas with a coolant problem, where it was rescued by 66099. This turned out to be the final farewell for EWS/DB Schenker Class 37s on the West Highland lines, as 37425 – the last member of the fleet in traffic – was withdrawn only days later.

Charter trains, including the luxury 'Royal Scotsman' and 'Northern Belle' operations, also continued to utilise Type 3 power to Oban and Mallaig as a result of route availability issues and they continue to do so today. Ever since EWS came into being following privatisation, its 37/4 fleet had a monopoly on these trains. Most charters, including the Edinburgh–Oban 'Northern Belle' workings, were hauled by a pair of locomotives, while the 'Royal Scotsman' only required one, except for between Fort William and Mallaig, where it would be 'top-and-tailed' by two. From late 2004, the 'Royal Scotsman' stopped hiring in EWS 37/4s and began using West Coast Railways (WCR) locomotives instead. The following year saw the 37/4 fleet dwindle in size considerably after more withdrawals, and the resulting lack of availability prompted the SRPS to follow suit and use WCR as well. Other charters continued to use them over the next few years until late 2009, when the fleet shrank to only two locomotives.

Liveries

Without providing an exhaustive list, it is fair to say that Class 37s working over the West Highland lines have carried a multitude of liveries. During their first few years of operation, all carried BR's 'corporate blue' colour scheme. Eastfield depot began tinkering with this livery from 1983 onwards, firstly when several 37s received bold white stripes painted along their lower body-sides.

The 'Scottie Dog' mascot also started to appear on locomotives at around this time. Furthermore, many of the split-headcode machines also had their headcode boxes painted black.

Eastfield depot became well known in railway circles as being one of the pioneering forces behind the move away from the BR 'corporate blue' image, with many other diesel depots in the UK starting to follow suit. In 1983, 37112 received extended yellow ends around its cab-sides: a more basic form of the 'Large Logo' livery which became commonplace over the next few years (a livery first conceived south of the border on Class 56s). As well as extended yellow ends, 'Large Logo' included black window surrounds, large BR double arrow logos, light grey roofs and large 'Scottie Dogs'. As well as 37/0s, this livery was carried y all of the 37/4s, many of which eventually received black-painted headcode panels: namely 37401-6/8/10-2/25.

In 1988, 37423 was repainted in the then new Railfreight triple grey colour scheme, before shortly after receiving Trainload Metals vinyls and its *Sir Murray Morrison* nameplates. 37401 then became the first of the class to receive InterCity 'Mainline' black/white/red colours. Between 1989 and 1990, most other 37/4s received this livery, with the rest either painted in Railfreight Distribution (37403/13) or Trainload Petroleum (37428) triple grey. The only exception was 37408, which would retain its 'Large Logo' for several years. As for the 37/0s, those which were still extant in the West Highlands in the early 1990s were repainted in Civil Engineers' Department 'Dutch' grey/yellow livery.

The galaxy of liveries in abundance following privatisation included Railfreight triple grey, but with TransRail logos added. Interestingly, 37403 received the *Ben Cruachan* nameplates from 37404 and was repainted into original BR green livery with small yellow warning panels to commemorate the centenary of the West Highland main line in 1994. On the other hand 37425 made many appearances on the line during the latter part of the decade in the attractive blue/white livery of Regional Railways. Meanwhile, the 37/0s and 37/5s carried all kinds of liveries in the 1990s, the main ones of which are detailed below:

BR	blue
BR Departmental	Civil Engineering 'Dutch' grey/yellow (with or without TransRail logos)
InterCity	'Swallow' black/white/red stripe
LoadHaul	orange/black
Mainline Freight	'Aircraft blue'
EWS	maroon/gold

One particularly interesting locomotive was 37116 *Sister Dora*, which had flush front ends and carried BR blue, but with TransRail logos. Meanwhile, the 37/6s all carried triple grey livery but with European Passenger Services (EPS) logos.

As the 2000s took hold, the dominant livery on the West Highland lines was EWS maroon and gold. There were two forms of this – initially it used large arial font 'EW&S' logos and latterly Gill Sans font that read simply 'EWS', but with the 'Three Beasties' cab-side logo added. Most of the 37/4 fleet received one of these styles, together with many 37/0, 37/5 and 37/7s. However, in 1998, 37428 received a special claret livery to match the coaching stock of the 'Royal Scotsman', when it was chosen as the prime locomotive for hauling this prestigious train.

Later years saw 37401/16 also painted in 'Royal Scotsman' colours, but without the gold lining seen on 37428. Number 37401 received the name *The Royal Scotsman*, replacing 37428 as the dedicated locomotive for the train, which itself unusually received the old nameplate *Loch Awe* on one side and *Loch Long* on the other. All three locomotives had the special 'Royal Scotsman' coat of arms emblazoned as a metal plaque on their body-sides but 37401/16 lost these during their latter days in service. All West Coast Railways locomotives carry a similar claret livery to match the luxury train, but with old BR-style half-yellow warning panels.

All EWS Class 37s retained the company's maroon/gold house colours after the takeover by DB Schenker, with the exception of 37419/670, which were repainted in the scarlet red/grey livery of their new employers. Both received small 'DB' stickers on their headcode panels. While 37419 ended up being withdrawn after only one outing in the new colours, 37670 put in a couple of months' service on charter work, including working the Edinburgh–Oban leg of the 'Northern Belle' luxury train, before being put into store.

The DRS Class 37 fleet carries the company's dark blue colour scheme, which, along with WCR maroon, is now the dominant livery on West Highland 'Tractors'. However, there have been one or two exceptions to the main liveries listed above in recent years. Number 37425 was repainted into BR 'Large Logo' by EWS in 2005 to commemorate the end of loco-hauled passenger trains in Wales and put in several appearances on engineers' and MoD traffic in 2010. Another noteworthy example was West Coast Railways' 37261, which carried BR Brunswick green, complete with working headcode panels. It appeared as a standby locomotive at Fort William in 2004 for the 'Jacobite' steam train, before an eventual repaint into WCR's house colours.

The Class Today

Since the withdrawal of the remaining EWS/DB Schenker locomotives, the only Class 37s to be seen on the West Highland lines have been DRS or WCR examples. Charter trains over the lines employ locomotives from both companies and with more of them being reinstated into traffic or fitted with RETB, which

With a snow-capped Ben Challum dominating the backdrop, DRS Class 37/4 No 37419 *Carl Haviland* approaches Crianlarich from the Fort William line with a Bridge of Orchy–Mossend empty 'Autoballaster' on 28 February 2013. The train had been held at Upper Tyndrum for around forty-five minutes to cross a ScotRail Sprinter. The Up points set indicator for Crianlarich station can be seen to the right of the track. (Author)

1. The same Class 25-hauled train featured on page 49 is seen crossing another northbound train, this time at Arrochar & Tarbet. The train on the right is headed by an unidentified Class 27, as the secondman and signalman exchange tokens. Note the elegant subway entrance and signal box. June 1980. (Allan Trotter, Eastbank Model Railway Club)

3. Uniquely-liveried Class 104 DMU No 104325, AKA the 'Mexican Bean', waits at Crianlarich before departing on a shuttle service to Oban on 3 August 1986. (David Webster)

2. Ardlui has been a regular crossing point for Sprinters in recent years. Often one service has to wait around five minutes for the other to appear, with several passengers stepping out to the platform for a cigarette! On 18 February 2002, 156485 leads the combined morning train from Oban/Mallaig while 156478/457 wait with the 0812 Glasgow–Oban/Mallaig. Note the sprinkling of snow on 156485's cab front. (Author)

4. 21 January 1989 was the penultimate day of loco-hauled trains in the West Highlands before Class 156 Sprinters were introduced. In dismal weather, Trainload Metals-liveried 37423 *Sir Murray Morrison* accelerates away from Tyndrum Lower with the 1204 Glasgow Queen Street–Oban. (David Webster)

5. LNER K4 No 3442 *The Great Marquess* and K1 No 2005 approach County March Summit with a very late-running West Highland Centenary Special on 7 August 1994. While the K4's apple-green livery is authentic, the Peppercorn-designed K1 was built in 1949, so never carried these colours prior to preservation. (Jules Hathaway)

6. A wintry scene on 14 January 1989 sees 37402 *Oor Wullie* and 37408 *Loch Rannoch* approaching County March Summit from the north with the 0840 Fort William–Glasgow. The name *Oor Wullie* was eventually given to 37275 instead, while *Loch Rannoch* was originally carried by 37012. (David Webster)

7. 'Black Five' No 45407, this time disguised as former classmate No 45487, crosses the southernmost viaduct of the Horseshoe Curve near Tyndrum, with a special photographer's charter on 17 October 2010. Note the line bending sharply in the background across the second viaduct. (Bob Avery)

8. The upper slopes of Ben Dorain are shrouded in shadow as GBRf's 66735 hauls the 6E45 0807 Fort William–North Blyth empty alumina tanks between Bridge of Orchy and Tyndrum on 24 June 2013. The train is about to reach the Horseshoe Curve, where the Class 66 will have to slow to 20mph to cross two viaducts. (Author)

9. Another interloper to the West Highlands – Class 50 No 50049 *Defiance* (with 50031 *Hood* on the rear) – powers away from Bridge of Orchy at the head of a Pathfinder Railtour returning from Fort William on 6 March 2005. The tour reached Mallaig and was originally booked to take in Oban as well, but Network Rail prohibited this at the last minute. (Jules Hathaway)

10. The scores of photographers out to capture the final few weeks of Class 37 haulage on the 'Caledonian Sleeper' certainly had the weather gods on their side. On 6 May 2006, 37417 *Richard Trevithick* growls uphill from Bridge of Orchy with the 0450 Edinburgh–Fort William. (Bob Avery)

11. Threatening storm clouds gather across Rannoch Moor, as Class 37/4s Nos 37423 *Sir Murray Morrison* and 37419 double-head the heavy 7D60 1430 Fort William–Mossend 'Enterprise' past Milepost 62½ between Rannoch and Gorton loop. The locomotives carry the liveries of TransRail and EWS respectively, while the wagons are mostly loaded with paper from Corpach. (Jules Hathaway)

12. Not long after the Fort William sleeper had been saved, 37430 *Cwmbrân* crosses Rannoch Viaduct with the 1900 Fort William–London Euston on 18 June 1995. The train is conveying no less than four Mark 3 sleeping cars, likely due to the huge swell in passenger numbers which occurred around the time the service was threatened. (Jules Hathaway)

13. As the evening sun disappears behind the surrounding hills, DB Schenker Class 67 No 67004 shatters the peace in the Monessie Gorge with the 1950 Fort William–Edinburgh 'Caledonian Sleeper' on 25 June 2013. Southbound trains face a continual climb the whole way from Fort William Junction to Corrour Summit. (Author)

14. The original Fort William motive power depot was clearly in its death throes by the time this photograph was taken in April 1968, with the former steam shed now missing its roof. As well as two North British Type 2 diesels, a Class 08 shunter can just be made out in the background. The vacuum-operated turntable has actually been preserved and is operational today at Kidderminster on the Severn Valley Railway. (Allan Trotter, Eastbank Model Railway Club)

15. The classic view of what is probably the most famous railway structure in the world: Glenfinnan Viaduct. The unique Stephenson link motion 'Black Five' No 44767 *George Stephenson* heads the northbound 'Jacobite' on 10 July 1997. (Jules Hathaway)

16. BR-liveried 'Black Five' No 45407 *The Lancashire Fusilier* storms past the remote church Our Lady of the Braes, Polnish, on 26 June 2013, with the 1015 Fort William–Mallaig 'Jacobite'. Owned by Ian Riley and based at Bury on the East Lancashire Railway, the Stanier 4-6-0 has been a regular main-line runner for most of her preservation career. (Author)

17. Since 1984, steam locomotives on the West Highland Extension have typically always returned tender-first from Mallaig. LMS-liveried No 5305 *Alderman A.E. Draper* is pictured skirting the east end of Loch Dubh on her way back to Fort William on 30 August 1987. She is heading a 'West Highlander' land cruise which originated at London St Pancras. (Tom Noble)

18. On 26 June 2013, Class 156 Sprinters 156499/492 rattle across Loch nan Uamh Viaduct with the 0903 Glasgow Queen Street–Mallaig. Both units carry the latest ScotRail 'Saltire' livery. (Author)

19. Class 55 'Deltic' D9009 (55009) *Alycidon* heads the 1Z63 1823 Oban–Fort William leg of the Deltic Preservation Society's 'Freedom of Scotland' railtour across the Orchy Viaduct near Loch Awe, on the beautiful evening of 25 June 2003. 55019 *Royal Highland Fusilier* was positioned at the rear of the train. (Jules Hathaway)

20. Sprinter 156478 draws into Taynuilt on 25 May 2013 with the Summer Saturdays 1611 Oban–Glasgow. Note that Ben Cruachan, 3689ft-high in the background, has had trees cleared along its slopes. Timber used to be transported from the goods sidings to the right of the picture. (Author)

has resulted in a large variety of different sub-classes being used. All of the WCR fleet, first used on the 'Royal Scotsman' in 2005, are 'no heat' examples: a mixture of 37/0, 37/5 and 37/7. This means that trains operating outside the summer months require a generator car for train heat and power (including the 'Royal Scotsman'). The steam-hauled 'Jacobite' also requires a standby diesel locomotive, usually a WCR 37, while severe snowfalls over the line in recent years have also seen the fleet used for light engine 'snow patrol' runs; their three-piece miniature snowploughs being useful for clearing the line.

The DRS Class 37 fleet is expanding rapidly and currently consists of machines from sub-classes 37/0, 37/4, 37/5 and 37/6. Many are RETB-fitted and a good number have been extensively refurbished, with modern light clusters at each end. It is pleasing to report that the company are gradually returning a number of the ex-EWS 37/4s to traffic as well; their Electric Train Supply (ETS – formerly known as ETH) proving useful for charter work. The DRS fleet cover a variety of duties on the West Highland lines. The charter traffic includes working the 'Northern Belle' between Edinburgh and Oban.

In addition, DRS now supply 37s for use on test trains, inspection saloons and engineers' workings over the Oban and Mallaig lines. It is the ballast trains in particular that have proved popular with photographers and these turns have used various members of the fleet. Number 37419 *Carl Haviland* made some notable appearances during February 2013, which included a layover at Oban on 20 February and a rare visit to Mallaig on 26 February. Even more remarkable was the use of 37419 and 37688 *Kingmoor TMD* double-heading a train of long-welded rail from Mossend to Ardlui on 21 February. This was the first double-headed 37-hauled freight in the West Highlands for several years, though it unfortunately ran during the hours of darkness.

At the time of writing, the familiar English Electric growl of the Class 37 can happily still be heard in the West Highlands, albeit no longer on a daily basis the way it once was. Class 66s are still barred from the Oban and Mallaig lines due to their route availability issues and, as yet, there are no signs of these problems being resolved, meaning that 37s should still hold sway on engineers' duties for a while yet. The same applies to many of the charter trains for the same reason. And with DRS having recently reinstated a number of the ETS-fitted 37/4s into traffic at the time of going to press, there is every chance that this trend could continue for some time.

The 37s have achieved something of a cult following among diesel enthusiasts and have developed a strong association with the West Highlands in particular. Indeed the Friends of the West Highland Lines used to have the image of a 37 on their company logo, such was the way they had become etched into the fabric of the lines. The distinctive sound of their exhaust beat reverberating around the glens was once very much an everyday sound in the area, often heard for a full ten minutes after the train had disappeared from view – a glorious auditory spectacle! But over and above that, the 37s have always been dependable and useful machines, popular with crews, and they provided a reliable passenger service for twenty-five years.

Class 66

The new millennium saw a new, unfamiliar shape appear on West Highland railway metals: the Canadian-built General Motors Class 66. Replacing Class 37s on freight traffic, the '66s' would soon become a common sight at all corners of the UK rail network.

Amid a wild mountain landscape, GBRf's 66737 *Lesia* climbs Glen Falloch with the 6S45 0635 North Blyth–Fort William loaded alumina train on 28 February 2013. This is one of the many areas where line-side trees have been recently cleared thanks to the Friends of the West Highland Lines. (Author)

Factfile

Power type:	Diesel-electric
Builder:	General Motors, London, Canada
Build date:	1998–present
Total produced:	446 (as of 2014)
Wheel configuration:	Co-Co
Engine:	General Motors/EMD 12N-710G3B-EC
Weight:	126 tonnes
Maximum tractive effort:	92,000 lb
Brake force:	68 tonnes
Max speed:	75mph
Route availability:	RA7
Nickname(s):	Sheds, Ying-Yings

Sub-classes Used on West Highland lines
66/0
(66001-250)   EWS/DB Schenker fleet
66/7
(66701-749)   GB Railfreight (GBRf) fleet

Story of the 66s
When the English Welsh & Scottish Railway (EWS) was created in 1996, it inherited a large locomotive fleet of various classes, in various conditions. Modernisation was inevitable and this came in the shape of 250 new diesel locomotives ordered to replace many of the older designs such as Class 31s and 37s. The new diesels – Class 66s – were introduced into traffic between 1998 and 2000, resulting in a mass cull of the existing locomotive fleet.

The 66s, despite being billed as 'modern' locomotives, actually took on a design conceived back in the mid 1980s on the Foster Yeoman Class 59s. The 66s retained the '59' bodyshell and had similar but updated General Motors power units. Intended purely for freight use, the 66s had no train heat capability and were numbered 66001–250. From 1998, they soon spread their wings all over the British railway system, rapidly becoming established in Scotland on coal and 'Enterprise' wagonload freight work. Their high reliability was a great benefit to EWS, although diesel enthusiasts were far from pleased because they replaced the popular Class 37s, and these disgruntled folk called them 'Red Death'!

Even the traditional switchback Glasgow–Fort William line would soon see the introduction of the class but first some clearance issues would have to be resolved. The 66s weighed 126 tonnes, with a Route Availability of RA7, while the 37s already in use were just 107 tonnes and RA5. The Craigendoran–Oban/Fort William/Mallaig routes all had a maximum clearance of RA5. Nevertheless, EWS and

Railtrack began negotiations to get the big Type 5s passed for operation between Craigendoran and Fort William. Approval for their use was eventually granted, but only after several underbridges along the route were strengthened to cope with their weight. Even with the work, the 66s still had speed restrictions of as low as 10mph across certain structures, and these were still in force at the time of writing.

Despite this development, no such clearance was given for the 66s on the Oban and Mallaig lines, even though EWS still operated timber traffic to Taynuilt. It was also notable that the class were not permitted over the short section between Fort William Junction and the town's station, due to the bridge over the River Nevis being in a poor state of repair.

During the latter half of 2000, Class 66s started to take over from 37s on most of EWS's West Highland freight flows. The Mossend–Taynuilt and Fort William–Corpach workings were the exceptions, though the class would soon be passed to run as far as Corpach too. Motherwell Traction Maintenance Depot created a dedicated pool of locomotives (coded WBBM) that were fitted with RETB equipment for working the West Highland and Inverness–Wick/Thurso lines, comprising of 66095–114. From new, all members of the class had been fitted with self-steering bogies – ideal for the severe curvature of the West Highland main line.

Over the next few years, the same locomotives, 66095–114, were regulars over the Fort William road. Unfortunately though, the RETB-fitted fleet could not be used to their full potential, thanks to the drastic reduction in freight over the line in 2001. The daily return alumina working between North Blyth and the Fort William Alcan plant was for some time their only daytime duty, latterly becoming an 'Enterprise' working to/from Mossend. And after a spell of night-time operation, the 66-hauled Mossend–Arrochar/Crianlarich timber trains ceased to operate in late 2006.

The class were also utilised for occasional engineers' traffic between Craigendoran and Fort William. Number 66107 even defied the 66 ban on the Oban line when it surprisingly worked a Mossend–Dalmally 'Autoballaster' on 13 February 2008 – the first and so far only appearance for the class on the former Caledonian Railway route. The Type 5 had been given special dispensation to work the train after the failure of 37422, despite 66s not being officially passed to operate on the route.

The highest numbered of the RETB-fitted 'Sheds', 66114, had the distinction of twice rescuing the 'Caledonian Sleeper' after Class 37 failures. On 21 April 2004 it worked the northbound 1Y11 with a failed 37427 between Corrour and Fort William. Earlier, on 1 November 2002, it hauled a failed 37401 on the same train as an empty coaching stock move after the train was terminated at Tulloch. Note that by this time 66s had been passed to run into Fort William station. Railtours have also provided rare passenger haulage for the class, the first of which was Pathfinder Railtours' 'West Highlander' hauled by 66104 from Mossend to Fort William on 10 April 2009 and then southwards to Preston three days later. Number 66114 was back in passenger action again on a UK Railtours excursion on 23 May 2011, when it top-and-tailed with 66111 between Dumbarton Central and Crianlarich.

Following engineering work south of Crianlarich, Sunday 3 March 2013 saw two empty ballast trains head north to Fort William Junction Yard during the afternoon. With ten JJA 'Autoballasters' in tow, 66107 creeps slowly across Auchtertyre Viaduct in Strath Fillan with the first of these workings. (Author)

After EWS was taken over by DB Schenker, early 2010 saw the '66/0s' largely give way to GB Railfreight's (GBRf) '66/7' fleet on West Highland freight work. This was following GBRf's acquisition of the contract for the Alcan alumina traffic. A special driver training run in preparation for the new workings was made to Fort William on 13 February 2010, with 66728 *Institution of Railway Operators* hauling a pair of Class 325 Royal Mail EMUs to simulate the wagon load. This made for a very unusual sight, rattling across the wilds of Rannoch Moor on a cold winter's day!

While EWS/DB Schenker's 66095–114 were permanently fitted with RETB sets, the 66/7s carry portable units, which can be switched around regularly from locomotive to locomotive. 66734 *The Eco Express* was the first of the sub-class to be withdrawn from traffic after being involved in the Loch Treig derailment on 28 June 2012.

Since early 2010, the DB Schenker 66/0s have been seen far less often on the West Highland main line, with their only remaining booked diagram becoming the weekly Mossend–Fort William oil train. This, together with the closure of Motherwell TMD and the reduction in freight traffic north of Inverness, means that the RETB-fitted batch of 66/0s are no longer necessarily concentrated in Scotland and can be found working all over the UK on all kinds of traffic.

One would hope that West Highland freight can expand again so that the Class 66s could gain new work, other than the oil and 66/7-hauled alumina trains which are the only diagrams at the time of writing. It might even allow the big General Motors machines to finally get the all-clear to run to Oban and Mallaig, both of which are currently still out of bounds for the class.

Liveries and Modifications

The 250 66/0s were all originally delivered in EWS maroon and gold livery with a zig-zag pattern along the body-side. Painting of the fleet into DB Schenker livery has been a slow process, with only those locomotives requiring major works attention receiving the new colours. This livery is scarlet red in colour, with a low, grey body-side stripe and partly-grey roof. 'DB Schenker' is applied on the body-sides, with small 'DB' stickers on the cab fronts and much smaller body-side numbers than those in EWS livery.

GBRf locomotives have had several livery variations. The initial one was dark blue and orange, still carried by some locomotives into 2010. Number 66705 carried a large Union flag painted on its body-sides to accompany its name *Golden Jubilee*, applied in June 2002. On the other hand, 66709 *Joseph Arnold Davis* formerly carried a black-and-orange version of the main GBRf livery, advertising GBRf's shipping company, Medite.

After the First Group took over GBRf, many locomotives received the company's house colours of blue with white/pink trim, similar to the First ScotRail Sprinters. This provided the first chance in a long time to see passenger and freight trains operating alongside one another in near-matching livery on the West Highland lines. After First Group sold the company to Europorte in 2010, this was replaced by a new version of the original GBRf blue-and-orange livery, utilising a lighter shade of blue with new 'GB Railfreight' logos on the cab-sides. Locomotives 66718–722 carry this livery but with 'Metronet' branding for use on London Underground infrastructure trains, though they have also visited the West Highlands.

A real blast from the past has been the application of 'West Highland Terrier' motifs on Class 66s. These were most noticeable on GBRf's 66725 *Sunderland* and 66728, which carried them for short periods. EWS/DBS's 66111, on the other hand, has for a long time carried Inverness 'Highland Rail' yellow stag emblems on its body-sides.

A very noticeable difference between many 66s is the style of lights fitted. There are three styles: the original three-lens WIPAC clusters, two-lens WIPACs with bright LEDs, and a larger style with two bigger LEDs. The early style WIPACs are used on the 66/0s, while GBRf's 66/7s carry all three variants.

Class 67 No 67004 calls at an immaculate Spean Bridge station at 0938 on 26 June 2013, nearing its journey's end with the overnight sleeper which left London Euston at 2115 the previous evening. In recent years, the 67s had the eighth notch in their throttles isolated to show DB Schenker's dedication to reducing their carbon footprint. (Author)

Class 67

Introduced in 2006 on the 'Caledonian Sleeper' service, General Motors Class 67s have become an everyday sight on the Glasgow–Fort William West Highland Line. Their use on the line – in spite of a high axle load and the severe speed restrictions that entails – highlights ScotRail's commitment to providing a highly reliable passenger service for years to come.

Factfile

Power type:	Diesel-electric
Builder:	General Motors, sub-contracted to Alstom (Valencia, Spain)
Build date:	1999–2000
Total produced:	30
Wheel configuration:	Bo-Bo
Engine:	General Motors/EMD 12N-710G3B-EC
Weight:	88–90 tonnes
Maximum tractive effort:	32,000lb
Brake force:	68 tonnes
Max speed:	125mph (80mph RETB-fitted locomotives)
Route availability:	RA8
Nickname(s):	Skips

The Caledonian Sleeper

In 1998, the English Welsh and Scottish Railway (EWS) ordered a fleet of thirty new diesel locomotives capable of 125mph running to replace Class 47s on mail trains. Enter the Class 67 – built on foreign soil to modern specifications similar to the freight-only Class 66, but with added Electric Train Supply (ETS) for hauling passenger trains too. All thirty locomotives entered traffic during 2000.

After only three years of being bedded into traffic, in 2003 Royal Mail announced that the company would cease to use rail transport completely. This resulted in the withdrawal of all postal trains and in effect making the Class 67s redundant. As a result, the next few years would see EWS find use for the class on other traffic. Since 2000, ScotRail had been hiring a 67 each night for use on the Edinburgh–Aberdeen portion of the 'Caledonian Sleeper', followed in 2001 by their introduction on the Edinburgh–Inverness section. The Edinburgh–Fort William leg remained Class 37-hauled, but it was widely speculated that this too could see 67s in the near future.

ScotRail's intention to use 67s on the Fort William 'beds' became quite clear when they carried out a trial run on 4 October 2003, with 67004 *Post Haste* hauling a rake of six coaches from Edinburgh to Fort William. Although the trial was said to be successful, moves to introduce the 67s were not forthcoming. The problem lay mostly in their heavy axle load, with the class being classified RA8 and therefore not passed to operate over the RA5 West Highland Line. However, it was determined that, like the Class 66s, the 67s *could* still operate, albeit with restrictions.

This meant that they would be required to slow down to 20mph to cross most bridges and viaducts along the route. A 10mph restriction was enforced over three of the structures – Auchtertyre and Garelochhead Viaducts, and Underbridge 341 crossing the River Nevis at Fort William. A maximum restriction of 40mph over the whole line was also put in place for the 67s. However, the trial with 67004 had established that the class's swift acceleration meant that the time lost en route through speed reductions was negligible.

Following the trial run in 2003, ScotRail and Network Rail took some time to consider their options with regards to 67s operating in the West Highlands, but it was widely expected to be just a matter of time before they were introduced. That day finally came on 10 June 2006 – over two-and-a-half years later – when 67004 hauled the 0450 Edinburgh–Fort William (1Y11). EWS created a small, dedicated pool (WABN) of locomotives fitted with RETB equipment to haul the train, made up of 67004/7/9/11/30 and also including 67008 until July 2006 only.

However, the introduction of 67s on the 'beds' was far from seamless and problems arose immediately. The very first run on 10 June reached Fort William over two hours late due to a multitude of faults, including defective brakes, ETS and RETB, plus other minor issues. The same train had arrived bang on time at Edinburgh the night before behind 37405, which told its own story! The months that were to follow saw a number of instances of late running on the 1Y11/1B01 sleepers, with the word going about that drivers were struggling to keep time on account of all the speed restrictions faced by the 67s. There were also occasional failures which saw Class 37s return.

One particular problem noticed early on was that the 67s' brake blocks were being worn down very quickly, due to the amount of braking required on the West Highland main line as a result of the speed restrictions, gradients and tight curves. The brakes were having to be changed virtually every week until EWS found a solution. Eventually during 2007, all of the RETB-fitted machines were fitted with a special type of brake block designed to withstand this damage: a composite material of cast iron and steel. This reduced their overall top speed to 80mph but solved the braking problem.

By this time, most difficulties with the locomotives had been resolved and their performance on the sleeper had improved significantly. From a driver's point of view, one great improvement they had over the 37s was their computer-controlled anti-wheelslip mechanism – especially useful during the autumn leaf-fall season in the West Highlands.

Other Traffic
The Class 67s – since their introduction on the sleeper in 2006 – have seldom been used on any other duties in the West Highlands. This is partly attributed to the fact that they are not clear for running over the Oban line or west of Corpach on the Mallaig line. The occasional railtour in recent years has utilised the class, as has the odd freight turn. At the time of writing, they have appeared on both the Mossend–Glen Douglas MoD trains and the oil traffic to Fort William. Time will tell if they are to be passed to operate to Oban and Mallaig – if so, then this will open more doors for the class.

Numbers and Liveries
All of the RETB-fitted 67s were painted in the Class 66-style EWS maroon/ gold 'zig-zag' livery from new. In time, it is expected that all will be repainted into DB Schenker's red/grey livery. Number 67013 *Dyfrbont Pontcysyllte*, painted in silver 'Wrexham & Shropshire' livery, was a rare visitor to Fort William between 24–25 June 2011, when it powered the 'Three Peaks Challenge': a special charter organised for hikers travelling across England, Wales and Scotland. The locomotive had to be fitted with a portable RETB set for the journey north of Helensburgh Upper. In addition, several other non-RETB-fitted 'Skips' have been employed on the 'Northern Belle' on the occasions it has terminated at Helensburgh Upper.

Also of note in more recent years has been the application of small stickers (only visible up close) on the cab fronts of many locomotives, with at least some of the RETB-fitted examples receiving Scottish saltire flags.

The Class Today

After a slippery start, the 67s have now settled into their West Highland passenger role rather well. Many rail fans will lament the passing of Class 37s on the sleeper service, but it is difficult to argue against the new locomotives from an operator or everyday passenger's point of view. Through time they have proved themselves to be reliable and powerful machines – not to mention being more environmentally friendly, with less noise and carbon emissions than their predecessors. More than anything, their introduction may well ensure that the sleeper service continues to be viable – very important for the future of the West Highland lines.

Class 156 'Super Sprinter'

The Class 156 DMUs are a familiar sight to anyone visiting the West Highland lines today, dominating all passenger workings to Oban, Fort William and Mallaig. Designed with operational simplicity in mind, ideal for rural routes, the Sprinters replaced loco-hauled trains in 1989.

Factfile

Power type:	Diesel Multiple Unit
Builder:	Metro-Cammell (Washwood Heath, Birmingham)
Build date:	1987–89
Total produced:	114
Formation:	2 cars per set (DMSL + DMS)
Engines:	Cummins NT855R5 (one per car)
Weight:	DMSL 36.1 tonnes, DMS 35.5 tonnes
Max speed:	75mph
Route availability:	RA1
Nickname(s):	Sprinters

Early Years

The Class 156s were part of the new wave of DMUs built by BR in the 1980s to oust locomotive-hauled trains, known as 'Second Generation DMUs'. They were a development of the Class 150 Sprinters which had taken over many regional passenger services south of the border, but intended for many of the longer distance routes. Built by Metro-Cammell in Birmingham between 1987 and 1989, the 156s were two-car units designed to work in multiple if necessary, featuring gangway end doors and a Cummins 285hp underfloor engine in each car.

The customary splitting of a northbound service at Crianlarich on 28 February 2013 sees First ScotRail-liveried 156485 head off for Oban on the 0821 from Glasgow. 156474 waits at the platform with the Fort William portion. (Author)

The Class 156s were given the moniker 'Super Sprinters' by BR (usually shortened to Sprinters); part of a marketing initiative to highlight their superior acceleration to the trains they were replacing, which would reduce journey times as a result. On top of that, they were designed to economise, because they did not have the same running costs and maintenance issues associated with loco-hauled trains. A typical example of this would be the ability to split trains en route, which meant that there was no longer the need to run separate trains from Glasgow Queen Street to Fort William and Oban respectively. Locomotive run-rounds and complicated shunting would also be eliminated.

The West Highland lines managed to remain Sprinter-free throughout 1987–88 despite Class 156 introduction elsewhere in the UK. However, the writing had been on the wall for some time and the January 1989 timetable change saw Class 37s give way to the new DMUs on the Glasgow–Oban/Fort William/Mallaig circuit. The first official day of the new trains was Monday 23 January, though a pair of 156s actually made a surprise appearance the previous Friday on a 37 diagram.

The 156s were operated by BR's 'Provincial' sector, which later became known as Regional Railways (under the ScotRail banner). The units used on West Highland diagrams were based at Edinburgh Haymarket and the allocation was initially made up of 156445/7/9/50/3/6. Individual coach numbers for each of the units began with a '52' or '57' respectively, meaning, for example, that set number 156445 would be formed of cars 52445 and 57445. All of the units allocated to the West Highland lines had RETB equipment fitted, along with small single-piece snowplough/obstacle deflectors at each end. They also had automatic sliding doors and hopper-type windows.

Most winter-time workings would see the 156s operating a two-car service to Oban and two cars to Fort William/Mallaig, with trains joining or splitting at Crianlarich. Their first summer on the West Highland lines in 1989 saw the Haymarket-based units converted into three-car formations to reduce overcrowding. Sets 156435/99/500 had their cars donated to the middle of 156445/7/9/50/3/6 for this purpose. This practice was repeated during the summer of 1992, though generally individual portions either ran as two- or four-car formations through the years. This meant that combined six-car formations became a regular sight south of Crianlarich, with longer trains not being permitted due to the short platform lengths en route. That said, there have been one or two records of eight-car formations before!

First ScotRail's 156457 pauses at Garelochhead with the four-car 1821 Glasgow–Oban/Mallaig service on the evening of 24 April 2011. The main building and signal box may be boarded up, but the station is otherwise in a very presentable condition. The Class 156 still carries the old style of lights fitted to the class, which were replaced soon after. (Author)

The three-car formations in 1989 and 1992 were dispensed with at the end of the respective summer seasons. The reintroduction of a few summer Class 37-hauled trains to Oban, Fort William and Mallaig from 1992–94 increased the availability of the rather stretched Sprinter fleet and allowed them not only to aid capacity on other Scottish routes but to double up more frequently too. Most of the units used on the West Highland lines had been transferred from Haymarket to Glasgow Corkerhill depot earlier in 1992, which already had a sizeable allocation of the class for use around Glasgow and south-west Scotland.

The 1990s was a solid period for 156s in the West Highlands, which had impressed so far with their excellent reliability record in the first few years. RETB equipment had been added to other members of the class earlier in the decade to strengthen the West Highland fleet and by 1996, 156436/45/7/9/50/3/6/65/85/92-96/500 could all be seen working north of Craigendoran. It was not until 1997 that full privatisation of the Regional Railways ScotRail sector took place, which saw National Express's ScotRail franchise take control of the fleet; they operated them for several years, right up until First Group took control in 2004.

There was little in the way of change for the 156s throughout this period, bar the repainting from the erstwhile Provincial livery to new ScotRail colours. For a few years in the late 1990s, two of the class ran with names closely associated with the West Highlands: these were 156465 *Bonnie Prince Charlie* and 156449 *Saint Columba*. These were removed when the units received the new ScotRail livery.

The 2000s saw the Sprinters continue to provide an ongoing reliable service in the West Highlands. First ScotRail now operate the fleet, which is still based at Corkerhill and, at the time of writing, is made up of fifteen sets: 156447/50/3/6-8/65/7/74/6/8/85/93/9. Various units have carried RETB equipment over the years, with some having it removed at various stages. Therefore, as well as the class members mentioned earlier, other RETB-fitted 156s that have, or may have, worked over the West Highland lines include 156430–2/4/5/7/9/42/62/504/5.

One notable change on 156s from 2006 onwards was the implementation of digital destination displays at each end, replacing the original roller blinds. More prominent was the 2012 addition of new light clusters to all of the First ScotRail fleet. These each have two lenses as opposed to the previous three, using bright LEDs, and have altered the units' front-end appearance significantly.

The Class 156 Sprinters have provided a very reliable service on the West Highland lines from day one, though opinions are still mixed regarding their suitability for such long distance, scenic journeys. First ScotRail summer workings from 2011 have seen some Oban and Fort William trains run as separate services to/from Glasgow, allowing longer train lengths, so now is probably the best time to view the class in this part of the rail network. There are no plans to displace them as yet, but time will tell if the Sprinters are to survive for another two decades.

Liveries

All 156s originally allocated to the Oban/Fort William/Mallaig routes carried BR's Provincial sector light grey/light blue/dark blue/white livery, with 'Super Sprinter' branding. These colours ruled throughout the 1990s, but with the 'Super Sprinter' logos replaced in 1994 by much smaller ScotRail logos on the run-up to privatisation. The units survived in this condition for the rest of the decade. However, the Strathclyde Passenger Transport Executive's allocations of Sprinters based in Glasgow had their own colours – in the late 1990s this was an attractive carmine-and-cream livery as applied to BR's coaching stock in the 1950s. At least 156430 and 442 are known to have been interlopers on the West Highland lines whilst in this livery.

From mid-2000, ScotRail's 156s in the original Provincial livery were repainted into a bright new ScotRail colour scheme of white/terracotta/aquamarine/purple, with larger ScotRail 'Whoosh' logos on the body-sides. From late 2004, when ScotRail was taken over by First, most units were initially given First-branded ScotRail logos replacing the 'Whoosh' brandings on both body-sides and cab ends. This was an interim measure, with all units receiving new First Group 'Barbie' livery over the next few years. This is primarily dark blue, with white-and-pink trim.

At the time of writing, First ScotRail's Class 156s are gradually being repainted into new dark blue colours, with First logos replaced by the legend 'ScotRail: Scotland's Railway'. All of the West Highland fleet are expected to receive these colours eventually.

Others

Aside from the previously mentioned types of locomotives and multiple units that were or still are commonplace on the West Highland lines, there has been a large variety of other types of motive power seen since the beginning of the diesel era. Some of these have been interlopers more usually associated with other regions on the BR network, while some classes have seen short periods of regular use.

The 350hp **Class 08** diesel shunters had, for a long time, an important role behind the scenes around Fort William, where they were used entirely for local shunting duties or short trip workings. Following the end of steam, the locally-based J36 0-6-0s were replaced by an 08 to carry out the same type of work; the trip workings including short trains to both the local aluminium smelter and the recently opened Corpach paper mill. A shunter would continue to be based here until early in the 1980s, when these duties instead became the preserve of the versatile Class 20s.

Between 1989 and 2000, an 08 was once again outbased at Fort William Tom-na-Faire depot, usually working between there and Fort William Junction Yard, whilst trip workings were in the hands of Class 37s. Individual locomotives used varied through the years, though perhaps the most memorable was former Eastfield depot pilot 08938, which carried a very personalised version of Railfeight grey livery with large 'Scottie Dog' emblems and the boldly-painted depot code 'ED' on the body-sides! Other 08s known to have spent periods at Fort William since 1989 were 08630/720/35/853/910/36. Sadly the class disappeared from the scene altogether at the start of the new millennium, when it was decided that a local shunter was no longer required, ending a long-time railway tradition in Lochaber.

Eastfield depot had an allocation of the Sulzer **Class 25** Bo-Bos during the late 1970s, which primarily saw use in central Scotland but were also used to supplement Class 27s on workings to Oban, Fort William and Mallaig. They often double-headed with their BRCW-built (Birmingham Railway Carriage and Wagon Company) counterparts on the heavier passenger workings,

The rare appearance of a Class 25 at Mallaig, with ex-works 25109 seen running round a service for Fort William in June 1980. Its appearance this far west is probably due to a locomotive shortage at Eastfield depot, which typically occurred around May or November time when there were reallocations for the respective summer or winter timetables. Incidentally, 25109 was part of the 25/2 sub-class and did not carry a train heat boiler. (Allan Trotter, Eastbank Model Railway Club)

being similarly powered with a relatively low axle load and thus well-suited to the West Highland lines. Typical locomotives seen between 1975 and 1980 were 25005–14/49/84–7/230–33, all allocated to Eastfield depot. They were transferred to Glasgow to replace **Class 24s** – a type always very scarce in the West Highlands.

The last Class 25s were withdrawn from ordinary BR service around the same time as the 27s in mid 1987, though three of them were converted into ETHEL units to provide Electric Train Heat for the Fort William sleeper service. The locomotives in question, 25305/10/4, were renumbered as 97251/50/2 (named *ETHEL 1,2 & 3* respectively). After the Electric Train Heat-fitted '37/4s' arrived on the scene, the ETHELs were made redundant but found new work providing heat on steam-hauled specials throughout the BR network. Repainted into InterCity livery, they saw occasional use providing heat on the Fort William–Mallaig steam-hauled trains in 1988, much to the displeasure of steam enthusiasts. In 1992, the ETHELs were withdrawn from stock and scrapped two years later.

Class 26s were another type commonly associated with other routes in the Highlands but scarce in the west. However, they were the only Scottish-based Type 2 class to survive into the 1990s (until 1993) and ScotRail allowed them to sign off in style, utilising them on a number of specially organised passenger workings during their last few years in traffic. Numbers 26001 (named *Eastfield*) and 26007, became celebrity locomotives when they were painted into their original BR green livery in August 1992 to commemorate the closure of Eastfield depot later in the year. Returned to their original condition, they received their original numbers D5300 and D5301, complete with headcode discs and large 'Scottie Dog' depot plaques.

ScotRail arranged a special railtour running from Edinburgh to Oban on 12 July 1992, intending to use the two green '26s'. It turned out that their repaints were not completed in time, so the tour utilised 'Dutch'-liveried 26025 and 26026 instead. However, problems with 26025 continually shutting down resulted in some late running and 26026 hauling the five-coach special on its own for long periods! On the return journey, the pair were swapped at Dumbarton Central for 26036 and 042. The two celebrity machines – 26001 and 007 – were completed in time for a repeat of the same run on 23 August, which was more successful, despite problems with the multiple-working system resulting in the locomotives being driven in tandem between Helensburgh and Oban.

One of the 'pilot scheme' batch of Brush Type 2 locomotives participated in trial runs between Glasgow and Mallaig in 1958, being one of the first diesel designs to be used in the West Highlands. These were later re-engined and re-classified as **Class 31** – a type never common in Scotland. However, one of the gifts of the privatised railway is that it paved the way for more unusual traction to reach the more remote outposts. This included the '31s', which started to make occasional railtour forays to the West Highlands from the 1990s onwards. Then in 2000, a surprise move by West Coast Railways saw the hiring of 31190 *Gryphon* from Fragonset Railways to act as a standby locomotive for the 'Jacobite' steam train over the summer. It was used several times to cover for steam failures and also saw use on four of Fragonset's own excursions – running twice from Fort William to Mallaig and twice from Fort William to Oban, billed as the 'Flying Kipper' and 'Flying Haggis' respectively!

Number 31190 was stationed at Fort William again in summer 2001, with 31128 *Charybdis* performing the same duty the year after. The standby contract with Fragonset ceased after this, but there was a brief flurry of 31 action in the West Highlands again in the summer of 2005, when a locomotive shortage saw 31190 and 31602 *Chimaera* hired by West Coast Railways to work the 'Royal Scotsman'. This saw 31+37 combinations running to Taynuilt and Mallaig, and even the two 31s double-heading, with 31190 now in the colourful Railtrack livery. Aside from these duties, 31s have also visited the West Highlands occasionally on Serco or Network Rail test trains.

Class 33s were another type completely alien to Scotland never mind the West Highlands, though West Coast Railways' small fleet of 33025/9/207 have seen occasional use in recent years. From 2006, they started making regular appearances on the 'Royal Scotsman' – receiving permission to work despite having a route availability of RA6. They also made appearances on empty coaching stock workings to Fort William for WCR and had periods stationed at Fort William as standbys for the 'Jacobite'. Their period of association with the West Highland lines, 2006–08, even saw 33025 and 029 gain the names *Glen Falloch* and *Glen Loy* respectively, formerly carried by the famous 'Glen' class steam locomotives; a move that certainly turned a few heads. Number 33207 even had a week stationed at Fort William to act as a snowplough standby locomotive during the Big Freeze of December 2010.

The date of 25 August 2007 marked the first appearance of a **Class 40** on the West Highland lines, with the Class Forty Preservation Society's 40145 *East Lancashire Railway* working an SRPS railtour from Carlisle to Fort William. The Type 4 was fitted with a portable RETB set for this purpose, in common with all locomotives making 'one-off' appearances on the lines. The class's route availability of RA6 had previously prevented them from working here in BR days.

Class 47s, despite being such a ubiquitous class in Scotland for many years, were barred from the West Highlands under BR as they were classified as either RA6 or RA7. This barrier was broken on 9 November 2002 when 47798 *Prince William* and 47799 *Prince Henry* top-and-tailed the Royal Train to Spean Bridge, where the Duke of Edinburgh was visiting. From mid 2005, West Coast Railways'

Fragonset Class 31s Nos 31601 *Bletchley Park 'Station X'* and 31602 *Chimaera* pass the site of Oban Goods Junction with a joint A1A Charters/Railtours Northwest Wigan–Oban railtour on 24 June 2000. At Oban station, the two locomotives had to run round the train separately, as the front wheel of 31602 was overshooting the point blades by about 18in. (Jules Hathaway)

own fleet of 47s became regulars on railtours to Fort William and Mallaig, typically top-and-tailing most trains. The 'Royal Scotsman' also became a regular duty, except for on the Oban line which had always been out of bounds for the class. WCR mostly uses ETS-fitted '47/7s' and '47/8s', painted in the company's maroon livery to match the 'Royal Scotsman'.

Class 50s made their first appearance on the West Highland lines on 4–6 March 2005, when preserved 50031 *Hood* and 50049 *Defiance* worked between Swindon and Mallaig on Pathfinder Railtours' 'Monarch of the Glen' excursion. Both locomotives were naturally adorned with 'Scottie Dog' motifs for the occasion.

A **Class 55** 'Deltic' ran for the first time on the lines on 2 August 1981, when 55021 *Argyll and Sutherland Highlander* headed a BR 'Merrymaker' excursion from Edinburgh–Oban. It repeated this run three weeks later on 23 August, this class being suitable for the line with route availability RA5. Preserved 55019 *Royal Highland Fusilier* made the class's first appearance at Fort William on 4–5 March 2000, working a Regency Rail excursion originating at Cardiff.

Then from 24–26 June 2003, the memorable Deltic Preservation Society 'Freedom of Scotland' railtour saw 55019 and 55009 (D9009) *Alycidon* top-and-tailing to visit Oban, Fort William and Mallaig. Since then, mainline regular 55022 *Royal Scots Grey* has hauled various charters to all three termini. However, its finest hour came on 30 May 2011, when by special arrangement it worked the Fort William–North Blyth empty alumina train for GBRf.

Recent years have seen the occasional use of WCR's **Class 57** prototype 57601 on railtour and 'Royal Scotsman' work – the first of a class of re-engined and refurbished '47s'. WCR also acquired the ex-Freightliner '57/0s', with some seeing use working the Western tour of the 'Royal Scotsman'. Furthermore, the Virgin Trains' '57/3s' unusually had a short spell working timber trains from Chirk to Crianlarich and Arrochar from 2007–2008, operated by the equally short-lived AMEC-Spie railfreight company. It was even more surprising when, on 16 March 2010, Virgin's 57301 *Scott Tracy* was used to haul the southbound alumina empties after a Class 66 failure.

While the West Highland lines succumbed to diesel power in the 1960s, earlier than many other routes, it took a long time for diesel multiple units (DMUs) to become established in the area. **Class 101s** were one of the 'First Generation' DMUs which saw use for a few years. Until the mid 1970s they had a regular out and back summer-only diagram between Glasgow Queen Street and Oban. This was worked initially by the Swindon Cross-Country **Class 120s**. The '101s' have also seen use over the line more recently in departmental use, such as Network Rail's 960002 *Iris II* – which was a '101' converted for video survey work, though it has now been withdrawn.

The West Highland routes were entirely locomotive operated in the 1980s until halfway through the decade, when ScotRail introduced the Crianlarich–Oban summer shuttle utilising the 'Mexican Bean' **Class 104** unit 104325 (car numbers 53424 and 53454). Its striking maroon-and-white livery was enhanced further by early BR-style 'speed whiskers' on the cab fronts and advertising slogans painted on the body-sides (reading: 'Scotland's for me!' and 'The Scottish Highlands and Islands'). Also featured were 'Scottie Dogs' – initially in the small size but printed much larger by 1986. A headboard 'Spring into Oban' was also carried at the beginning of these operations. Every so often during the summer the 'Mexican Bean' would return to Eastfield depot for refuelling and maintenance, and it was transported to and fro on the rear of the main passenger trains. It sat out the winter months at Cowlairs carriage sidings. After working its third and final season in 1987 it languished at Thornton Yard in Fife for a short time before being scrapped.

Various other DMUs have made occasional visits to the lines – they were either on test, special workings or in departmental use. Eastfield depot had a former Class 122 single car unit renumbered as TDB977177, used during the mid 1980s for applying sandite to the rails to aid adhesion during the autumn months. Prototype diesel-electric multiple unit 210001 made an appearance during the 1980s, as well as one of the prototypes for the Sprinter units, 150001. The latter unit was the basis for the Class 150s, which established themselves in Scotland but never on the West Highland lines. However, Network Rail's track assessment unit 950001, purpose-built but to the same design as a Class 150, has made several appearances in more recent years. The Class 121 'Bubblecars', formerly owned by Railtrack, have also visited on departmental use.

6

Steam Renaissance

The celebrated 'Jacobite' steam operation on the Fort William–Mallaig line today owes its very existence to a venture started by British Rail back in 1984. BR ran the trains every summer from 1984–94, when Carnforth-based company West Coast Railways took over following privatisation. 2013 marked the thirtieth anniversary of workings – consecutive workings at that, as steam has returned every single summer since the inaugural year.

Despite becoming a private enterprise, the set-up has changed little over the years. Two (occasionally more) locomotives have always traditionally arrived

One of the many Stanier 'Black Fives' which have graced the West Highland lines in the preservation era, LMS-liveried No 5305 *Alderman A.E. Draper* tops the County March near Tyndrum on 17 October 1987 with an SRPS railtour. This was the first steam-hauled train over the Glasgow–Fort William line since 1963. (David Webster)

from south of the border at the beginning of the summer, complete with their own dedicated set of coaches, and taken turns operating the train throughout the season, normally working boiler-first to Mallaig and tender-first back to Fort William. Then at the end of the summer the engines and stock return back south.

BR agreed to give steam a try in 1984 following the popularity of its experimental diesel-hauled Sunday excursions between Fort William and Mallaig. Preserved main-line steam had already become well established despite BR's strict policy, with the Steam Locomotive Operators' Association's (SLOA) regular programme of specials over the Settle & Carlisle route, showing there was potential for more of the same elsewhere. Three different locomotives were brought to Fort William for use that summer: ex-LMS Stanier Class 5 4-6-0s Nos 5407 and 44767 *George Stephenson* and North British Railway 0-6-0 'C' class No 673 *Maude*. Fort William's Tom-na-Faire depot became the base for the operations and has continued to serve that role ever since.

One of the few preserved 0-6-0s to have been main-line certified in the UK, No 673 *Maude* was owned by the SRPS and latterly classified as one of the J36 class carrying the BR No 65243. Members of this class were ever-present at Fort William during the days of steam. *Maude* worked a four-coach special operated by the SLOA on Monday 28 May 1984, booked to run from Fort William to Mallaig before No 5407 hauled the first public BR train that same day.

In the event, the train ended up terminating at Arisaig after the 0-6-0 had struggled with the West Highland gradients and lost too much time. There were further problems on the return journey, with *Maude* having to stop at the edge of Loch Dubh to take water using a portable pump! Sparks from her exhaust had also started a number of line-side fires along the route and caused signalling cable to be burned, adding to the delays. It was realised after this that *Maude* was too lightweight a locomotive for hauling any decent load to Mallaig, so she was instead given a few Fridays-only two-coach trips between Fort William and Glenfinnan. She did, however, double-head to Mallaig with No 44767 on the SLOA 'Lochaber' railtour on 1 September.

BR's own steam trips in 1984 operated every Wednesday, Thursday and Sunday, hauled by either one of the two 'Black Fives'. The 'West Highlander' was the name given to the service (not to be confused with the InterCity landcruise train of the same name), usually displayed on a headboard carried by the locomotive. No 44767 was a favourite amongst crews in the days of steam, with her unique Stephenson outside link motion carried since being built in 1947. Following the success of the first season, the locomotive returned for more summer duties on the Mallaig Extension in 1985, alongside No 5407.

Summer 1985 saw much wetter weather, but it was the first year that the steam trains used a special set of Mark 1 coaches that were to become a feature over the next few years. They were painted in a green and cream livery (based on the LNER Tourist stock of the 1930s), with 'Scottie Dog' motifs and the legends 'ScotRail' and 'West Highland' emblazoned on their body-sides. 1985 was also the first year that the 'Royal Scotsman' was steam-hauled to Mallaig, on Fridays.

'Black Fives' very rarely visited the Mallaig Extension in the days of steam, despite becoming regulars on the line south of Fort William after nationalisation. Smaller-wheelbase 2-6-0s were more ideal to crews, being better suited to the sharp curves and therefore less likely to suffer from tyre wear problems. It was this condition which started to affect the locomotives after some continuous use in the 1980s, exacerbated by tender-first running in one direction. This was unavoidable given that there were no turning facilities at either Fort William or Mallaig. Incidentally, 1985 saw No 5407 running boiler-first from Mallaig for the first few weeks only, before being taken to Glasgow for turning.

YEAR	LOCOMOTIVES USED, FORT WILLIAM-MALLAIG
1984	44767, 5407 (45407), 673
1985	44767, 5407 (45407)
1986	44767, 44932, 5305
1987	2005 (62005), 5305
1988	2005 (62005), 5305
1989	3442 (61994), 44871, 5305
1990	2005 (62005), 5407 (45407), 5305
1991	44871, 44932
1992	2005 (62005), 5407 (45407)
1993	2005 (62005), 44871, 44767
1994	2005 (62005), 3442 (61994), 44767
1995	48151, 75014
1996	44767, 75014
1997	44767, 48151, 75014
1998	48151, 75014
1999	1264 (61264), 48151
2000	61264 (1264), 75014
2001	61264 (1264), 62005 (2005)
2002	61264 (1264), 62005 (2005)
2003	61264 (1264), 62005 (2005)
2004	61264 (1264), 62005 (2005), 45407 (5407)
2005	61264 (1264), 62005 (2005), 45407 (5407), 76079
2006	45407 (5407), 48151, 5972, 61264 (1264), 62005 (2005)
2007	45231, 45407 (5407), 62005 (2005)
2008	45407 (5407), 45231, 62005 (2005), 76079
2009	45231, 45407 (5407), 62005 (2005)
2010	44871, 45231, 45407 (5407), 61994 (3442), 62005 (2005)

2011	44871, 45231, 45407 (5407), 61994 (3442)
2012	44871, 45407 (5407), 61994 (3442), 62005 (2005)
2013	44871, 45407 (5407), 62005 (2005)

The year 1986 saw No 44767 return for her third consecutive season, alongside a different '5MT', No 44932, which was notable for carrying BR lined black livery in a late 1940s guise with the lettering 'BRITISH RAILWAYS' on the tender. She returned home slightly early, on 24 September, to be replaced for the final few weeks by LMS-liveried No 5305 *Alderman A.E. Draper*, another of the eighteen preserved Class 5s.

No 5305 was to become a regular on the Extension over the next few seasons, as the steam operation grew from strength to strength, with revenue increasing by the year. She was joined in 1987 by the North Eastern Locomotive Preservation Group's (NELPG) LNER apple-green liveried K1 2-6-0, No 2005 – a very popular choice, of a class that were regulars over the line in the 1950 and '60s. A new set of Mark 1 coaches were also introduced on the service that summer, in the same green-and-cream livery, but this time just with the lettering 'West Highland Line'.

The continual success of the steam operation has always been thanks in no small part to the support crews of the locomotives and their preservation groups, who travel with their engines to Fort William for the summer to carry out all of the day-to-day maintenance. This includes emptying the smokebox and ashpan, starting or dropping the fire and carrying out repairs. The drivers and firemen during these first few years of steam were provided by BR, many of whom also drove diesel locomotives. On the rare occasions of a steam failure, BR normally provided a Class 37 diesel to haul the service.

While the Mallaig Extension was seeing regular steam haulage once again in the mid 1980s, no such trains had yet been operated over the line south of Fort William. The locomotives spending the summer based at Fort William were always hauled by a diesel to and from Glasgow at the start or end of the season, but this was about to change. On 17 October 1987, a return SRPS railtour from Edinburgh–Fort William saw 'Black Five' No 5305 haul the train south between Fort William and Craigendoran – the first steam-hauled train over the West Highland main line for twenty-four years. The run involved a stop near Corrour Summit, where the 4-6-0 took water from a nearby stream using a portable pump. A similar run was repeated by the SRPS to bring K1 No 2005 south on 14 November.

The year 1988 saw Nos 2005 and 5305 reappear once again for the summer season on the Extension, by which time the fitting of RETB equipment was mandatory for working the line. The two locomotives had portable radios and CDUs (cab display units) attached for this, which became the norm for all visiting steam locomotives from this point onwards. The 'Royal Scotsman' was still

With a headboard that reads 'The Flying Kipper', LNER K1 No 2005 is seen in charge of the 1105 Fort William–Mallaig just west of Glenfinnan on 1 September 1987. The green-and-cream coaches making up the train are part of the newer rake introduced in 1987, carrying the lettering 'West Highland Line' on the sides. (Tom Noble)

steam-hauled between Fort William and Mallaig in addition to the main trains, as was the InterCity 'West Highlander' land cruise.

The K1's return home at the end of the season was on a railtour on 19 November. However, the locomotive's support coach had to be removed from the train at Tulloch due to a hot axle box, which resulted in the 'special' running over two hours late as snow fell over Rannoch Moor. It was to become something of a tradition to run one or two steam-hauled SRPS railtours every autumn or winter for the next few years, as a gainful way to return the locomotives back home after a summer on the Mallaig line.

The steam season of 1989 was a thoroughly memorable one, with three different locomotives based at Fort William for much of the summer. K4 2-6-0 No 3442 *The Great Marquess* was a hotly anticipated visitor, being the only survivor from a small class that were built specifically for working the Mallaig Extension. Resplendent in LNER apple-green livery and normally based at the Severn Valley Railway, the mogul visited Fort William between 10 July and 5 August only, working the trains alongside 'Black Fives' Nos 44871 and 5305.

Seven coaches were normally employed on each train, such was the steam's popularity. The early workings in 1984 usually had five on, being increased to six for the next couple of years.

Instead of returning home following the summer season in 1989, No 5305 stayed on at Fort William until December, being retained by BR to train new drivers for the steam operation on several special empty coaching stock runs between Fort William and Mallaig. Her eventual return south was on 9 December, when she worked an SRPS railtour from Tulloch back to Edinburgh. Class 37 No 37424 had hauled the northbound trip and was supposed to have given way to No 5305 at Fort William. However, the train had ended up running very late due to RETB problems. A decision was eventually made to send the steam locomotive and its support coach to meet the train at Tulloch instead of Fort William, so as to claw back some lost time.

The last few years of the steam workings being operated by BR saw 'Black Fives' predominate and the green-and-cream coaching stock repainted, first into a rather incongruous InterCity colour scheme for a period, then into BR maroon livery. The icing on the cake for many enthusiasts was the appearance of LNER apple-green duo Nos 2005 and 3442 *The Great Marquess* on the 1994 centenary special, which then double-headed between Fort William and Mallaig on 9–10 August. This would be the last season of the BR-operated steam service, which during the last few years was named 'The Lochaber'.

29 MAY 1993, PAISLEY GILMOUR STREET– MALLAIG (RETURN), NO 44871 *SOVEREIGN*

Diesel-hauled south of Fort William (via Glasgow Central Low Level) both ways by 37232, 'Black Five' No 44871 took over this SRPS railtour at Fort William for the run to Mallaig and back. However, trouble lay ahead on the Beasdale Bank, where the Stanier 4-6-0 struggled to lift the seven-coach train up the 1 in 48 gradient before stalling completely. After reversing the train back some distance, another attempt was made at the climb. This time it came to a stand near Beasdale station and a decision was made to split the train in two. The locomotive duly headed the first three coaches as far as Arisaig before returning for the other four left down the line. The lost time resulted in the train being terminated at Arisaig, with the added complication that No 44871 had run short of water and had to run light to Mallaig to get her tender topped up. Diesel 37406 ended up being sent from Fort William to rescue the train, which didn't leave Arisaig for Glasgow until 7.45 p.m., meaning it was a very late bedtime for the passengers on board.

Number 44871 *Sovereign* stands at Arisaig on 29 May 1993 with her ill-fated SRPS railtour from Paisley to Mallaig. The train terminated here after the 'Black Five' had stalled on the Beasdale Bank, with the seven-coach train having to be split in two. (David Webster)

Early in 1995 there was uncertainty over whether that summer's steam programme would go ahead at all, with no new operator tied up. As well as high charges from Railtrack, there appeared to be no suitable locomotives, until the West Coast Railway Company (WCR) eventually stepped in with a new five-day-a-week set-up. The new 'Jacobite' trains would utilise another rake of maroon Mark 1s, hauled by two types of locomotive which had never worked over the Mallaig Extension in the days of steam. These were Standard Class 4MT 4-6-0 No 75014 from the North Yorkshire Moors Railway, and David Smith's Stanier 8F 2-8-0 No 48151.

The steam trains proved very popular during the early days of WCR operation, after some disappointing loadings latterly under BR. LNER green-liveried Thompson B1 4-6-0 No 1264 made a long-awaited return for her class to Mallaig in 1999. In October that same year, steam also worked to Oban for the first time since the 1960s, when 8F No 48151 headed a train organised by John Barnes's Highland Railway Heritage (HRH).

The Oban run was part of HRH's annual 'Highland Rail Festival', born in the late 1990s. Taking place every September and October, this was made up of a series of steam excursions over not only the West Highland routes but other lines such as the Highland Main Line and Inverness–Kyle of Lochalsh. Utilising the locomotives and stock from the 'Jacobite', the years 2000 and 2001 saw trains return to Oban again. The Thompson B1 had returned to Fort William in the summer of 2000, resplendent in BR lined black livery as No 61264 double-heading to Oban with No. 75014, which had received the name *Braveheart*.

Private photographic charters using the 'Jacobite' engines and stock also became a regular feature every autumn. Bob Branch's 26D Rail Recreations group organised these runs over both the Mallaig Extension and the main line to Glasgow. Special run-pasts and spectacular exhaust effects were added, allowing the most atmospheric of pictures to be taken by the scores of paying photographers.

The summer of 2001 saw the long-awaited reinstallation of a turntable at Fort William, at a cost of over £500,000 from the Heritage Lottery Fund. Seventy feet long and relocated from London Marylebone, it was placed in the sidings alongside Fort William Junction Yard and it was anticipated that a corresponding structure would soon be installed at Mallaig too, to be operated by the same group, the West Highland Railway Heritage Trust. The Mallaig project subsequently fell through, despite the fact that another turntable had actually been purchased.

One of the more unusual steam visitors to the West Highland Extension was Stanier 8F 2-8-0 No 48151 – part of a class which were never used in the West Highlands during the days of steam. On 26 June 1998, she is seen after arrival at Mallaig on the 1035 'Jacobite' from Fort William. For some time, the Crewe-built locomotive was to be seen in preservation carrying the name *Gauge O Guild*, seen here. (Jules Hathaway)

In the years that followed, the Fort William turntable ended up being rarely used, partly because it was not practical without one at Mallaig. There were also disputes about the charges to be paid for its use. Ever since, locomotives have generally only used this device for hauling private photographers' charters.

The year 2001 was also noteworthy for the appearance of both No 61264 and the NELPG's K1, which had also been repainted into BR black, as No 62005. The super-authentic sight of both locomotives hauling maroon Mark 1s was especially popular with photographers. It was also interesting that for this season No 61264 ran tender-first out of Fort William.

Prior to the beginning of the 2003 'Jacobite' season, the northbound empty coaching stock move on 12 June – headed by Nos 62005 and 61264 – was involved in a minor collision with the 1300 Oban–Glasgow service train at Glen Douglas. Two-car Sprinter 156478 scraped the rear carriage of the train at the southern end of the crossing loop, though neither derailed. It was due to the nine-coach steam train slightly overshooting the loop, where it had arrived to await the passage of the DMU. The only major damage was to the door of the affected Mark 1 coach and, after a thorough examination, both trains were allowed to proceed with the rest of their journeys a few hours later.

The popularity of the 'Jacobite' increased considerably thanks to the *Harry Potter* films, with various promotional material highlighting the fact that the train used the same coaching stock and travelled through the same locations as seen in the films. For enthusiasts, there was the added bonus that WCR continued to arrange for BR-liveried locomotives to haul the 'Jacobite'. After an absence of several years, the 'Black Fives' have returned, with No 5407 a regular performer since

6 OCTOBER 2001, FORT WILLIAM–OBAN, NOS 62005 & 61264

Only the third visit of steam to the Oban line since the 1960s, there was naturally plenty of local interest in this charter (practically the whole population of Dalmally turned out to witness the train's passing!). Operated by Highland Railway Heritage, it saw the two ex-LNER locomotives unusually working tender-to-tender, which allowed the K1 to head the train south from Fort William and the B1 to head towards Oban. Unfortunately the train was delayed for some time at Crianlarich due to RETB problems after the engines had run round. Its eventual arrival in Oban allowed it to be in position for the following day's departure back south, returning Nos 62005 and 61264 and the WCR 'Jacobite' coaching stock back to Carnforth for the winter.

27 OCTOBER 2012, POLMONT–FORT WILLIAM (RETURN) NOS 44871 & 45407 *THE LANCASHIRE FUSILIER*

This was the first SRPS special in a long time to use steam power on a southbound run from Fort William and it also marked the welcome return of double-headed 'Black Fives' to the West Highland main line, for the first time since the 1960s. The train was hauled northwards by WCR diesel 47804, with Nos 44871 and 45407 attaching to the train at Fort William together with their two support coaches, taking it up to load eleven. The two Stanier 4-6-0s gave a rip-roaring performance all the way back to Polmont, though there were bouts of slipping at times, resulting in the Class 47, which had been shadowing the special on the southbound leg, being added to the rear at Crianlarich to assist.

2004 in BR guise as No 45407. Sister engine No 45231, yet another member of the eighteen class members preserved, has also spent several recent seasons at Fort William. Both locomotives carry the preservation-era nameplates *The Lancashire Fusilier* and *The Sherwood Forester* respectively.

Nowadays, several different engines tend to be used on the 'Jacobite' throughout a whole season as opposed to just two, the way it used to be. Often two have been based at 'The Fort' at once, with another locomotive arriving midway through the summer to swap over with one of the 'Black Fives' to ease their tyre wear problems. Standard Class 4 mogul No 76079 has had a couple of forays over the Extension, running for a period as No 76001, which was a regular over the line in the early 1960s. *The Great Marquess* has also returned several times, especially on specials over the main line south of Fort William.

Even *Olton Hall*, AKA *Hogwarts Castle*, hauled the 'Jacobite' several times in July 2006, sending tourism into overdrive. The ex-GWR locomotive had once again been in the area for filming purposes and got a few run-outs on the train following the failure of B1 No 61264. But the real star performer in WCR days has been K1 No 62005, which has appeared almost every year from 2001–2013, despite having to be briefly stopped for an overhaul.

Such has been the surge in popularity of the 'Jacobite' in recent years, the service has expanded to operate seven days a week, with Saturday workings for most of June, July and August. With *Harry Potter* fever at its peak and trains regularly selling out, Saturdays became a regular fixture from the summer of 2007 onwards. The service was also gradually stretched to start in mid May and finish in late October – previously it only operated June–September. Though the pathing generally remained the same through the years, with a mid–late morning departure from Fort William and early–mid afternoon return from Mallaig.

With demand higher than ever in the 2011 season, clearly the existing seven-coach 'Jacobite' could have been longer if it hadn't been for the gradients and short crossing loop lengths. It was a defining moment in the history of the steam operations when a *second* daily train was added to the roster – running with a different locomotive and coaches in a later afternoon slot. This resulted in the thrilling sight of both steam-hauled trains passing one another at Glenfinnan.

'Black Five' No 44871 (now minus the *Sovereign* nameplates carried in the 1990s) was the designated locomotive for the new afternoon train that summer, hauling an air-braked set of WCR Mark 1 and Mark 2 stock, while the K1 handled the main service.

Glenfinnan is the only place on the national rail network where two steam-hauled trains regularly pass one another. On 26 June 2013, Stanier Class 5 No 44871 waits with the afternoon 'Jacobite' to Mallaig while sister engine No 45407 *The Lancashire Fusilier* arrives with the morning service. (Author)

The afternoon train has returned each summer since, running from June–August only, Mondays–Fridays. The two-train diagram, at the time of the 2013 season, was as follows:

2Y61	1015 Fort William–Mallaig
2Y62	1410 Mallaig–Fort William
2Y68	1430 Fort William–Mallaig
2Y69	1840 Mallaig–Fort William

The rest of the 2013 season saw the main train in operation Monday–Friday from 13 May to 25 October inclusive, and on Saturdays and Sundays from 22 June to 22 September.

Steam still appears regularly south of Fort William too. The year 2013 saw an appearance of the Railway Touring Company's annual 'Great Britain' special, which tours most rural lines in Scotland every April, hauled by *The Great Marquess* to Fort William and back. Occasional photo charters operate now and again, plus many engine or empty coaching stock movements as a result of the expanded 'Jacobite' set-up. Of course, all steam south of Fort William requires a lot of careful planning, including consideration for water stops, which has taken place at various locations over the years. Hydrants at Roy Bridge and Crianlarich have been used, as have road tankers at various stations, or even natural sources on Rannoch Moor. The 'Jacobite' locomotives, on the other hand, take water from a hydrant during layover at Mallaig.

ENGINES IN DISGUISE

If photographs were to be believed at first glance, one would think that over twenty-five different steam locomotives have operated over the West Highland lines in the preservation era. But the reality is that some have been given temporary number changes, or had names added, to assume the identity of some of their long-lost classmates, typically those based at Fort William shed in years gone by. Usually this has been for the purpose of special photographic charters. This has included 'Black Five' No 45407 running as No 44996, 45487 and 44908, 'B1' No 61264 running as No 61243 *Sir Harold Mitchell*, and 'K1' No 62005 as Nos 62012, 62034 and 62052. The latter also ran briefly as the unique 'K1/1' No 3445 *MacCailin Mor* whilst in LNER livery and for a long time carried the name *Lord of the Isles* whilst in BR black but still numbered 62005.

It is very pleasing to report that the steam service to Mallaig is at the very height of its success, having reached its thirty-first anniversary. In 1984, few would have imagined the huge scope of today's operations. But it is only thanks to the immense hard work of preservation groups, operators, locomotive crews and other volunteers that they have been able to reach this stage. Good publicity has also played its part. And as long as this continues, steam will continue to be a big part of the West Highland railway for years to come.

7

Passenger Traffic

Service Trains

From the late 1960s into the 1970s, Oban was served by four trains in each direction on weekdays. There was formerly a sleeper service to the town but this was lost to Beeching in the 1960s. One of the four trains a day was an overnight service without sleeping cars, leaving Glasgow Queen Street at 1 a.m., so timed to allow for an early morning ferry connection to the Isle of Mull, bringing in the morning mail and newspapers.

The early afternoon departure from Oban regularly had a parcels van attached to carry newspapers. Astonishingly, one occasional occurrence on this service for a few years in the 1970s was for an extra van to be added to carry corpses! The coffins would be carried all the way to Glasgow to reach funerals or the city mortuary. After all, rail was the quickest and most direct means of transport from Oban at the time, so the trains could really be used to carry anything and everything!

The Fort William–Glasgow service during this period was made up of three trains in each direction, with the Down morning and Up evening services both conveying sleeping cars to and from London Kings Cross. Between Fort William and Mallaig there were generally four in each direction, rising to five with an extra service that ran between April and October.

Following the introduction of '37/4s' in 1985, BR's Mark 2 coaching stock started to replace the earlier Mark 1s on all services. From October 1983, the Euston sleeper began using all air-braked stock, including Mark 3 sleepers and air-conditioned Mark 2s. The day coaches, including the 'air-cons', also formed the early afternoon return service from Fort William to Mallaig. The 1550 return, later changed to 1555, was the only through service between Mallaig and Glasgow. For some time the Mallaig and Glasgow lines had used separate trains, though the introduction of Sprinters would see most become through workings.

Throughout the diesel loco-hauled era, West Highland services varied in length. Winter trains could often be as little as three coaches long, or just two to Oban or Mallaig. By contrast, summer services regularly loaded to seven or eight. First-class accommodation, except for on the sleeper, was abandoned after January 1983. The 'Young Explorer' Class 37-hauled services during the early 1990s usually had a consist of three or four refurbished Mark 2 coaches in the attractive Regional Railways livery (with ScotRail branding). Interestingly, most of the workings from Glasgow–Oban/Fort William used Glasgow Queen Street low level station, though the Saturday trains in 1993 used the high level.

Following Sprinter introduction, the summer 1989 timetable saw year-round Sunday services to Oban, Fort William and Mallaig established. This marked the first time in the history of the West Highland lines there had been Sunday trains, except for the special summer excursions during the 1980s. Glasgow–Oban/Fort William had three trains in each direction on this day (excluding the sleeper), while Fort William–Mallaig had two – three including the steam-hauled service. Monday–Saturday there was the generous offering of four Sprinters each way on all three routes, involving the joining and splitting of Oban/Fort William portions at Crianlarich. Though there was initially a fifth Up train on the Mallaig Extension, which started its journey at Loch Eil Outward Bound at 6.30 a.m. bound for Glasgow. There was also a combined Mallaig/Oban service each way that was a through service to/from Edinburgh Waverley via Glasgow. ScotRail christened this service 'The Lord of the Isles'.

After 'Sprinterisation', the Euston sleeper was re-timed and operated for the first time as a stand-alone service. It became a Motorail service too for the first time, with cars being carried in GUVs, driven on and off the train from a loading ramp at Fort William station. The ramp is still in situ today despite the cessation of Motorail. The sleeper often had a load of seven coaches, including up to two GUVs and three sleeper vehicles, which were all soon painted into InterCity livery. Guards' accommodation was initially provided in a Mark 2 BSO coach, which was replaced in the mid 1990s by a BG full brake.

The four-train Sprinter service did not last, with Glasgow–Oban/Fort William services reverting back to three a day from October 1993. This general three-train pattern remained constant into the privatisation era, though there have been a few tweaks. October 1996 saw ScotRail introduce an early morning Monday–Friday commuter service from Garelochhead to Glasgow Queen Street, bringing back memories of the old steam era 'push-pull' workings. Proving to be useful for locals in the Helensburgh and Dumbarton areas working or studying in the city, 2005 saw it extended to start at Arrochar & Tarbet, departing at 0710 after running empty stock north. After stops at Garelochhead, Helensburgh Upper, Dumbarton Central and Cardross, it also pauses at several stations in the Glasgow area.

Another exciting addition to the summer timetable from May 2001 was a new Glasgow–Oban Saturdays-only return working, running from May to September. With a late-morning Queen Street departure and late-afternoon return from

A West Highland local train, twenty-first-century-style. The 0710 Arrochar & Tarbet–Glasgow, formed by 156485, stops for the early-morning commuters at Helensburgh Upper on 8 July 2013. The *Beeching Report* had originally been the death knell for the majority of similar services up and down the country. (Author)

Oban, it remains a popular train with holidaymakers. Furthermore, July 2010 saw a new Sundays Edinburgh–Oban return established once again to cater for tourists travelling from the east coast of Scotland, which has continued every summer since, running from the end of June until the end of August.

A look at the summer 2013 ScotRail timetable showed a wide number of variations. The most obvious was that of the morning services to Oban/Fort William/Mallaig and their afternoon returns. The respective Oban and Fort William/Mallaig portions ran as separate services to/from Glasgow, Monday–Friday, between 1 April and 25 October. On Saturdays, they ran as a combined train. Note that the operational period was now extended to take in the entire British Summer Time calendar. The Saturday extra to Oban and the 0956 Sundays-only from Glasgow (and return) also took in this extended period. Another happy 2013 development was the decision to make Falls of Cruachan a scheduled stop, as opposed to just a request stop, and also to have its opening period stretched from April to October.

Helped by massive hikes in petrol prices, patronage on the Oban services in particular continues to increase. The news that from May 2014 there would be twice as many trains running from Glasgow to Oban, with six services per day Monday–Saturday, was widely welcomed. This massive improvement comes after talks between ScotRail, Argyll & Bute Council and HITRANS (the Highlands and Islands Transport Partnership). It was initially proposed that five trains a day would run but huge demand resulted in a sixth getting the go-ahead.

New early-morning services, 0510 from Glasgow and 0520 from Oban, are designed to appeal to business travellers and schoolchildren. The 0520 ex-Oban will be the aforementioned Arrochar–Glasgow commuter train extended backwards to Oban. Morning/afternoon gaps will be filled by a 1037 ex-Glasgow and a 1441 ex-Oban. And a new 1637 ex-Glasgow will return from Oban at 2037 to provide a connection with the southbound 'Caledonian Sleeper' at Crianlarich.

The new services will be possible after the release of ScotRail Class 156s following the electrification of routes in the central belt. Among the various opportunities it will open up are improved connections to ferries and Oban airport, by changing at Connel Ferry. There are also suggestions that a new 'school service' could be implemented between Oban and Dalmally, with pupils receiving all-year-round rail passes.

Other recent timetabling improvements on the West Highland lines include the overnight sleeper now stopping at Dumbarton Central both ways, effective since the December 2012 timetable change. Dalmuir station, near Clydebank, has long been a booked stop for the service and is still a regular crew-change point. It has also been a booked stop for daytime West Highland services since the arrival of Sprinters.

The sleeper itself regularly fell victim to West Coast Route modernisation work south of the border during the early 2000s, when it was sometimes diverted or cancelled outright. One such period of engineering work on a few Mondays between December 2001 and February 2002 saw the northbound working advertised to run later in the morning. It turned out that passengers from London were transferred on to a Sprinter at Edinburgh for onward travel to Fort William – a great disappointment to the Class 37 aficionados!

FORT WILLIAM–LONDON EUSTON SLEEPER – 'THE DEERSTALKER'

Following the decision in 1995 to retain the Fort William sleeper service and its acquisition by the new ScotRail franchise under the 'Caledonian Sleeper' banner, the operation has changed little over the years. The Fort William portion of the train to/from London Euston is attached/detached from the Aberdeen and Inverness portions at Edinburgh Waverley station. The combined three portions run as a single service to/from Euston known as the 'Highland' service (the sleeper between Glasgow/Edinburgh-London is called the 'Lowland' train). The train departs from Fort William and London Euston every day of the week except Saturdays.

The Fort William portion has operated in and out of Edinburgh Waverley since 1991. After 'Sprinterisation' it operated out of Glasgow Central for a short period, then Carstairs, before Edinburgh. Its schedule has generally remained constant ever since, though the northbound service used to reach 'The Fort' around an hour earlier. Edinburgh is where the locomotive changes – a Class 67 (formerly Class 37) hauls the train between here and Fort William.

In recent years the train's formation has always included two Mark 2 seated 'day' coaches – a Brake Unclassified Open (BuO) and Restaurant First Open (RFO) – which are not part of the main train to/from London. During the night at Edinburgh, the Class 67 attaches/detaches these vehicles to shuttle between there and Fort William every day. Two Mark 3 sleepers (sometimes three at weekends) make up the rest of the short train. Formerly a Mark 1 BG full brake coach provided guards/luggage accommodation but these were replaced in 1999 by BuOs. Four coaches has generally been the norm on the sleeper since this time, when the rolling stock was repainted from InterCity livery into ScotRail purple and white. From 2005, the coaches were gradually updated into First ScotRail livery.

The Fort William sleeper still uses ScotRail drivers, even though the Inverness and Aberdeen portions use DB Schenker. The northbound 1Y11 reaches Fort William at 0955; still conveniently timed to connect with the morning 'Jacobite' to Mallaig. After arrival, the locomotive runs round the stock then shunts it into an adjacent siding, where the locomotive and carriages stable for the day. Here the stock is cleaned and serviced before departure in the evening.

Even without engineering work, delays south of Edinburgh have for a long time resulted in very late running of the sleeper on the West Highland section of its journey. There have also been rare occasions that it has been diverted to Oban instead of Fort William, sometimes due to line problems. This happened during two weekends in 2006 as a result of engineering work between Crianlarich and Fort William. Class 37 No 37406 hauled the return train on 11–12 February, while 37416 hauled it on 18–19 February.

Catering on West Highland services has been in the form of a trolley service ever since 'Sprinterisation'. Combined buffet-restaurant cars were abandoned during the late 1970s to be replaced by Mark 1 and 2 miniature buffet cars until the end of loco-hauled trains.

Luxury Trains

Thanks to the railway's huge scenic appeal, the West Highlands has been a popular destination for luxury land-cruise trains since the mid 1980s. The £3,440-per-head 'Royal Scotsman' is undoubtedly the pick of the bunch, still in operation today under Orient-Express Hotels Ltd – the same group that operate the 'Northern Belle' train. From 1985–1990, the train included various historic, pre-grouping era coaches, before a new rake of maroon-liveried stock was employed, mostly utilising Mark 1 Pullman vehicles. This now includes two Mark 3 sleeping cars.

The 'Scotsman' has traditionally always been run during the summer months – currently it operates April–October on a four-day 'Western Tour' between Edinburgh, Mallaig and Wemyss Bay. A single Class 37 was traditionally always the booked traction throughout the years, though the train was steam-hauled on the Fort William–Mallaig leg until privatisation. Latterly, EWS's (English, Welsh and Scottish Railway) specially-painted 37401/416/428 were the dedicated locomotives, though others often stood in. Top-and-tail working has become a regular practice north of Fort William, as the train is too long for the run-round loop at Mallaig. West Coast Railways locomotives have been hired to haul the 'Scotsman' since 2005, taking over from EWS. Classes 31, 33, and 37 have all been used on the train, though WCR now generally use a 47 or 57, with another locomotive (sometimes a 37) added to the other end at Fort William for the rest of the tour. ETS-fitted (Electric Train Supply) locomotives are not a requirement, as there is an on-board generator.

The four-day 'Royal Scotsman' Western Tour does not currently include the Oban line in its itinerary, though it did for many years, latterly as far as Taynuilt for an overnight layover. Though Oban is still served by sister train the 'Northern Belle', which operates sporadically during the summer. Double-headed EWS 37s provided the motive power until 2009, when the DRS 37s took over.

West Coast Railways' Class 57/0 No 57006 roars uphill past Whistlefield, near Garelochhead, with the 1333 Edinburgh–Spean Bridge 'Royal Scotsman' on 12 July 2013. This locomotive was originally built as Class 47 No 47187 before conversion to a Class 57 for use with Freightliner. (Author)

InterCity's 'West Highlander' land cruise ran to both Oban and Mallaig during the late 1980s/early 1990s, always hauled by an Eastfield/Motherwell '37/4'. It was usually made up of nine specially refurbished First Class Mark 1 carriages, including two catering vehicles, but no sleeping accommodation (passengers stayed overnight in hotels). This was in an era before top-and-tail operation became commonplace and run-rounds at Mallaig necessitated some complicated shunting, with the train being split in two!

Charter Trains

Charter train operations over the West Highland lines, both steam- and diesel-hauled, grew significantly during the 1980s and 1990s. And with more and more locomotives able to be fitted with portable RETB (Radio Electronic Token Block) equipment, and axle load restrictions relaxed, the new millennium has seen even more expansion. One of the most well-known tour operators is the SRPS, who have been involved for over three decades. As well as operating a number of the aforementioned steam excursions, their diesel-hauled tours to Mallaig formerly used a variety of vintage carriages, before the society had its own rakes of Mark 1s decked out in BR maroon. For a long time, 37/4s hauled most of the SRPS trains. EWS tended to use them in pairs, including top-and-tailing between Fort William and Mallaig. When the fleet dwindled in 2005, the SRPS started mostly using WCR Class 47s instead, as well as more exotic power such as 'Deltic' 55022 *Royal Scots Grey*.

The 1980s saw F&W Railtours, now Pathfinder Railtours, operate many 'Skirl o' the Pipes' multi-traction charters to Scotland. On 11 May 1985 this included a rare visit of Class 26s to Oban, when 26027/036 hauled the 'Skirl o' the Pipes 6'. Pathfinder has been one particular tour operator with a strong foothold in the West Highlands in recent years. In addition, the more recently established Statesman Rail now regularly runs its own Pullman trains hauled by WCR Class 47s.

Today there are probably more charter trains using the West Highland lines than ever before. A good day during the summer can see a couple of different specials on the Glasgow–Fort William line, not to mention the regular 'Royal Scotsman' workings. Capacity at the present Fort William station can be stretched during the summer, much like at the old terminus alongside Loch Linnhe. Especially now with everyday 'Jacobite' workings, an extra afternoon 'Jacobite', the 'Royal Scotsman', ScotRail services and whatever other charters happen to turn up! It is pleasing to report such activity over the lines, especially when one considers the many other scenic, rural railway lines in the country which see very few trains other than DMUs day after day throughout the year.

8

Freight Traffic

From the late 1960s and into the 1970s, general merchandise still accounted for a large amount of the freight traffic over the West Highland lines. Short-wheelbase open trucks and vans with brake vans were still commonplace until the 1980s, when Class 37s were introduced, and with them heavier, air-braked wagons. Loads of china clay (transported from Cornwall), pulp or finished paper to and from Corpach mill formed a large proportion of traffic through the decades. Until the early 1980s, these loads were generally carried in open wagons which were covered with hoods.

Bulk freight over the lines during the 1970s included oil, alumina, pulp and china clay, though mixed goods workings were still the order of the day. Timber and finished aluminium formed the rest of the loads on the main line to Glasgow. Coal was also conveyed to Oban and Fort William until 1983. Freight traffic was always generally lighter on the Oban line and by the 1980s, oil and timber were the only regular flows. As on the Fort William line, their main railheads in Glasgow were Cadder and Sighthill Yards, both latterly replaced by Mossend Yard. Mallaig's traffic levels were lighter still after the fish trains had finished – oil for the harbour's fishing boats was the only regular load by the beginning of the 1980s, operating once a week.

Following the cessation of pulp-making activities at Corpach, there were initially discussions about this side of the mill being reactivated at some point, but it never happened. By this time, Fort William was served by three regular freight trains in each direction per day. This pattern lasted for a number of years, save for a short period between 1982 and 1983 when the industrial disputes saw it cut to just two. A snapshot of these workings during the 1987 period was as follows:

Northbound
7Y31 0510 Mossend–Corpach
7Y37 1223 Mossend–Corpach
6S56 0712 North Blyth–Fort William

Southbound
7D10 0601 Fort William–Mossend
7D19 1223 Corpach–Mossend
6E46 1524 Fort William–North Blyth

A view from the window of a northbound train passing Corrour in June 1980 sees a Class 27 waiting in the loop with a freight from Fort William. The locomotive's number is not known, though it is one of the '27/2' sub-class which carried Electric Train Heating for passenger workings. The ETH jumper cable on its cab front is the giveaway. (Allan Trotter, Eastbank Model Railway Club)

The class 6 workings (6S56/6E46) were bulk alumina trains working out of the aluminium smelter, with the loaded wagons working north and empties south. The original style of hopper wagons used were replaced first by a more modern design in the late 1980s and then by the PCA tankers used today. The class 7 workings making up the rest of the daily freight were part of BR's wagonload network known as 'Speedlink'. Northbound loads conveyed pulp and china clay for Corpach paper mill, as well as oil for both Fort William and Mallaig. Southbound trains carried mostly sheeted paper from Corpach, timber and finished aluminium ingots, as well as empty wagons.

Mallaig (Fort William) Junction Yard was the point where the Speedlinks were shunted and the various wagons joined or separated. The oil tankers for Mallaig (usually three TTAs) were tagged on to the late-afternoon passenger service and returned empty the following day. Wagons for the aluminium works – and certain ones to Corpach – were carried there on trip workings, usually by the Class 20 yard pilot. The Class 08s originally used to take longer due to their low speed and, on at least one occasion, got stuck on Corpach bank! The 1990s saw Class 37s take over both these and the short oil trains to Mallaig. Also of interest was a short-term trial of fish traffic from Mallaig once again in March 1987, lasting several months.

Timber loading at Arrochar, Taynuilt and Crianlarich used specially converted OTA wagons, though some open types were used too. After being re-marshalled at Mossend Yard, loads were carried to a variety of destinations in the south over the years, including Irvine, Hereford, Chirk, Warrington and Welshpool. At Crianlarich, loading took place at the Down station sidings as well as the yard on the site of the former Lower station. By the 1980s, Oban's only regular goods consignment was fuel, latterly running on a thrice-weekly train to both the BP terminal adjacent to the station and Esso on the site of the former goods yard. This train also served Shell at Connel Ferry.

A large number of traffic flows were culled in the UK when the loss-making Speedlink sector was abolished in 1991, but thankfully it did not include any in the West Highlands. Operations instead became part of the scaled-down Railfreight Distribution. The train-crew depot at Fort William was at its busiest for some

The old and new order come face-to-face at Oban station on 2 September 1991. 37401 *Mary Queen of Scots* prepares to leave for Mossend Yard with a short rake of empty oil tanks from the depot on the quayside, while 156445 forms the afternoon service train to Glasgow. (Jules Hathaway)

time, though this would soon change as traffic was gradually lost. May 1995 saw the depot split following privatisation, with the ScotRail drivers moving to a new base at Fort William station.

The year 1993 saw the now-sporadic oil traffic to Oban, Connel Ferry and Mallaig cease to operate. It was the beginning of a downward spiral which would see the railway gradually fall out of favour with its customers, who saw road transport as a much cheaper and quicker alternative. This was despite much of the road network in the Highlands being, and still remaining to this day, completely unsuitable for heavy goods vehicles.

Following privatisation, TransRail, then EWS, took over the remaining freight. By this time there were just two daily trains to/from Fort William – one was the daily 'Enterprise' (the name given to modern day wagonload freights) to Mossend and one the bulk alumina tanks to North Blyth. The southbound 'Enterprise' originally ran as 7D19, the 0951 Corpach–Mossend, and was generally composed 50/50 of aluminium ingots and tarpaulin-covered rolls of paper, both bound for South Wales. China clay 'silver bullet' tankers from Burngullow in Cornwall were also sometimes conveyed.

Eventually the aluminium ingots transportation started running as a separate train, which in 1998 was taken over by Freightliner. Operating three times a week between Fort William and Coatbridge container terminal, a Eurostar 37/6

On hire to Freightliner from Eurostar, 37602 passes the remote Gorton crossing loop with the 7Y15 0845 Coatbridge–Fort William empty aluminium flats on 17 June 1999. (Jules Hathaway)

would be hired for two months at a time and out-based at Motherwell TMD (Traction Maintenance Depot) to haul it. The 7Y15 empties ran Saturday, Tuesday, Thursday, while the loaded 7D54 ran on Monday, Wednesday and Friday. Being a short train of only five or six KFA wagons, it was destined to be unprofitable and it was no surprise when it ceased to run at the end of the three-year contract in June 2001.

By contrast, the daily EWS 'Enterprise' was usually a very lengthy train in the late 1990s period and necessitated double-heading of Class 37s – typically two 37/4s or a 37/4+37/0 or 37/5. A typical consist would be nine or ten 'Cargowaggon' or Tiphook Rail vans, plus the odd china clay tanker. The northbound train (6Y45) was 0636 from Mossend and the southbound (7D60) was 1500 off Fort William. The southbound ran for a while as the through 7V60 1440 Fort William–Newport Alexandra Dock Junction. These became Class 66 turns latterly before the paper traffic ended in 2001, with the paper heading in containers to Italy for the intermodal company Ambrogio.

During the latter years of timber operation to Taynuilt, trains ran on an 'as required' basis as the 6Y42 0430 empties from Mossend and the loaded 6D55 1055 from Taynuilt. The same trains were occasionally extended to Oban for a period too, where wagons were loaded in the former oil sidings next to the station. From the summer of 2001, both sites were abandoned completely. In the case of Taynuilt, local complaints about noise and dust from lorries running through the village are believed to have played a part. Timber loading was also discontinued from the sidings at Fort William Tom-na-Faire depot.

This was part of a period of rationalisation for EWS's timber operations, which saw a new single 'pick-up' working to serve both Arrochar and Crianlarich during the night, with the wagons being loaded during the day. Operating Monday–Friday, it would run as the 6Y38 2055 Mossend–Crianlarich and 6D40 0233 return. Previously both destinations were just served on an 'as required' basis. Night operation now meant that there would be no booked crossings with other trains, so the timber could have extra wagons added. This continued until December 2006, when EWS pulled out of timber haulage.

AMEC-Spie railfreight's brief tenure in daytime timber haulage with Virgin Class 57/3s used bogie bolster wagons, then latterly the massive KSA type used today by Colas Rail. Since this traffic was discontinued in late 2008, timber has yet to return to the West Highland lines, with less demand today for paper production. However, much timber is still felled and transported by road in the surrounding area, particularly in Argyll. Road is seen as a far more viable option; less costly, coupled with the fact that using rail would still require the use of lorries to reach the loading yards anyway. However, the fact remains that running a single train can remove dozens of lorries from the narrow and twisty Highland roads.

The one flow which did survive relatively unaltered after 2001, the Fort William–North Blyth alumina, had its northbound path re-timed in spring 2004 to run as an 'Enterprise' between Mossend and Fort William, as it now also carried the occasional oil or china clay tanks. The new 6Y15 0826 Mossend–Fort William still returned as the 6E16 1758 from Fort William. Furthermore, finished aluminium ingots returned to rail in 2005 and EWS carried these on the daily 'Enterprise' too. It became a particularly lengthy train once again, especially on a good day with up to half a dozen oil tanks in the consist. For some time there had been discussions about reopening the oil sidings at Oban, Connel Ferry and Mallaig too, but in the end only Fort William saw traffic return. Corpach, on the other hand, was still served by irregular trip workings of china clay until the paper mill's complete closure in 2005. These were usually handled by the 37/4 rostered for the Caledonian Sleeper.

Shortly before GB Railfreight (GBRf) took over the bulk alumina traffic in early 2010, the finished ingots went back over to road transport, though oil remained the preserve of EWS/DB Schenker. The oil service has since run as a weekly 'as required' working (6Y15/6D16) between Mossend and the Scottish

With the surrounding mountains shrouded in mist, DB Schenker's 66105 climbs uphill towards Rannoch Moor at Achallader, with a Crianlarich–Fort William engineers' train on 3 March 2013. It is at this point that the A82 road and railway head off in different directions towards Fort William, with the road heading west via Glen Coe. (Author)

Fuels depot at Fort William, being anything from four to twelve TTA wagons. In addition, MoD trains still serve Glen Douglas admiralty sidings on an ad hoc basis.

The GBRf-operated alumina traffic between Fort William and North Blyth, on the Northumberland coast, represented a real positive step forward for West Highland freight operations when it began. The short twelve- or thirteen-wagon, five-day-a-week diagram previously run by EWS was replaced by much lengthier trains, now loading up to twenty-four wagons and operating three days a week. A typical loaded train weighs in at 1,176 tonnes while the empties are 455 tonnes. As track access charges are paid 'per train' and not 'per wagon', longer trains running less frequently are clearly more cost effective.

Alumina is the powdered raw material used to make finished aluminium, shipped from Ireland to North Blyth before being carried by train to Rio Tinto Alcan's Fort William smelter, where it is processed. The smelter has two sets of sidings – one next to the large storage silo where the tanks are unloaded and another where the ingots used to be loaded on to trains. Presently, loaded trains arrive on Tuesdays, Thursdays and Saturdays, with the empties leaving on Mondays, Wednesdays and Fridays, after the locomotive and train berth overnight at the factory. Access to the sidings is controlled by semaphore shunt signals and a ground frame, where a phone is provided to gain permission from the signaller at Banavie.

There continues to be speculation and proposals for new freight flows beginning on the West Highland lines. Amongst the various plans that fell through was one for the relaying of track at Crianlarich Lower to make it a timber loading yard once again, which was mooted during 2006. A plan which may yet see the light of day in the near future would see timber carried by rail from Rannoch Forest, on the southern side of the moor. As there are no nearby roads here, rail would be the only possible transport option, with loading taking place at night on the middle of the single track line. Trains would run north to Corpach, where BSW Timber now has a well-established sawmill on the site of the old paper mill.

Local haulage company Ferguson Transport also have a presence at Corpach, having opened a new depot next to BSW Timber in 2010, utilised by both lorries and ships in the adjacent harbour. The group already uses rail for part of its Corpach–Daventry flow – between Grangemouth and the south only, with lorries carrying containers from Corpach along the A82. Ferguson have long-term plans to use rail up to Corpach too, though the former paper mill sidings currently only stretch as far as the BSW Timber base. At the time of writing there are also suggestions that Tesco could be a potential new freight customer at Fort William, as they are at Inverness.

With regards to any future freight on the Oban line, or the Mallaig line west of Corpach, there is still one major stumbling block. Any new traffic would almost certainly require the use of Class 66s, which would only be possible with significant investment to strengthen a number of underbridges en route. But it appears Network Rail will only carry this out if there is a guarantee of traffic from one of the freight operators, for example DB Schenker. At the same time, the freight operator would want a guarantee from Network Rail that the line is suitable to handle their traffic. And so the issue goes round in circles.

While West Highland freight has been on a general decline since the 1960s, there is still hope for a revival. The loss of the paper mill which once saved the line has at least prompted the appearance and growth of the aforementioned new industries at Corpach. Time, and the economy, will tell if this results in a traffic upsurge, though the main line to Glasgow at least still remains an important freight artery for now.

9

Buildings and Infrastructure

Part of the appeal of the West Highland lines has always been in their well-kept and attractive items of infrastructure, such as station buildings. Most familiar trademarks of the old railway have remained, despite Beeching and RETB, though they are in various states of repair. Many stations now look more tidy and full of life than they have in a long time – partly thanks to the 'Adopt a Station' scheme run by ScotRail external relations manager, John Yellowlees. This involves ScotRail putting stations into the care of local volunteers, who restore or find new uses for buildings, and keep the area looking presentable, by doing gardening and other maintenance work.

The magnificently preserved station at Glenfinnan, where a small museum is centred around the main building. Its architecture and compact layout is typical of most of the original stations on the West Highland Extension, though Glenfinnan and Arisaig are the only ones to retain crossing loops. (Author)

Stations

The 'Swiss chalet'-style station buildings on the main line south of Fort William are one of the jewels in the crown of the West Highland railway. Most still remain in place today, especially the tiny signal boxes which carry the same style of architecture as the main buildings. When the line was built, nearly all stations between Helensburgh Upper and Spean Bridge had the same arrangement of main building plus platform-mounted signal boxes. The island platform layouts tended to have the box located towards the end of the platform, away from the main building, though visitors to Upper Tyndrum will notice that it has both buildings right next to each other, on the north end of the platform.

Glen Douglas, Gorton and Corrour were built with larger, more traditional signal boxes. Spean Bridge formerly had two boxes, but both were replaced by a new platform-mounted box in 1949, built to a flat-roofed LNER design. This distinctive building survives today in good condition; it is a Grade C Listed structure and was in use for many years as a greenhouse.

Stations with the 'Swiss chalet' architecture are today painted in original West Highland Railway green and cream colours with red brickwork; most of these were restored to this style during the 1990s. In the 1980s and the early part of the 1990s, most were painted in a North British Railway two-tone green colour scheme with red brickwork, though some were in lighter shades than others.

Buildings on the Mallaig Extension were also built to a distinctive style, generally smaller and more simplified compared to those south of Fort William. The larger style of signal boxes were designed by the Railway Signal Company for the North British Railway, though there were one or two exceptions. Lochailort had a very plain, brick-built signal box which closed in 1966, though survived in use as a bothy before it was demolished in 1986. There was also a box built at Annat in 1964, to serve a level crossing leading to the Corpach paper mill. It survived in use until 2011.

The Callander & Oban Railway, of course, had their own style, though Dalmally is the only surviving example of an original station building today. After years of neglect, the spacious, brick-built structure has been largely restored, complete with reglazed canopy, and is currently the headquarters of a local felt-making business. At Oban, the original large station building and canopy became disused in 1982, together with platforms one and two, when it was said to be unsafe. From then on, Oban took the form of nothing more than a simple branch line terminus, using only platforms three and four. It was here that a new main building was opened in 1986, with the old one being demolished.

Most station buildings and signal boxes went down the same road of dilapidation for some time after RETB, when they became unmanned. Crianlarich happily remained occupied thanks to the tea room located in one of the buildings.

Beasdale station lies at the top of the Beasdale Bank, which sees the railway climb at a vicious gradient of 1 in 48 north from Loch nan Uamh Viaduct. The original main building has long been out of use, though the station recently won a 'Keep Scotland Beautiful' Bronze award for its tidy appearance. (Author)

The original main building at the southern end of the platform was destroyed by fire and replaced by a modern waiting room many years ago. This too was eventually replaced in the late 1990s by a new structure – built to the original West Highland 'Swiss chalet' style. Arrochar & Tarbet also received one like this after its main building had to be demolished due to subsidence in 1999. Ardlui station lost its main building for the same reasons in the early 1970s.

Of the stations which retained their buildings and/or signal box, most fell into disrepair during the 1990s, with windows being boarded up and paintwork fading. Later in the decade, many were gradually restored to some degree. Bridge of Orchy has been restored to its former glory after the station building reopened in 2002 in immaculate condition as a bunkhouse. Its red platform chippings are also a longstanding feature of many of the West Highland stations. Rannoch has also been superbly restored in recent years, with its station building serving as a tea room during the summer months. Meanwhile, the signal box at Corrour lives on as a bunkhouse.

The stations on the Mallaig Extension are especially noteworthy, nowadays being very well maintained by volunteers such as the Friends of the West Highland Lines (FoWHL). Mallaig station received Gold status in the awards scheme 'Keep Scotland Beautiful' in recognition of its clean and tidy appearance, helped by floral displays. Other stations in the West Highlands have won Silver and Bronze awards.

Glenfinnan, too, is an absolute gem – beautifully preserved from top to toe. The station building is home to a small museum celebrating the history of the railway, run by John Barnes, who has gradually transformed the site over a number of years. In the small car parking area there is a former BR independent snowplough on display, as well as two former Mark 1 carriages, in use as a camping coach and cafeteria respectively. The refurbishment of the station in 2011 even went on to include that of the old signal box, which is fully intact with its levers still in place.

Permanent Way

Regular track maintenance has always been required on a daily basis to allow the West Highland lines to remain fully functional, especially so that they can handle heavy freight. Today this work is as important as ever (taking place day and night), though modern technology has made the job easier for the local permanent way teams, who are employed by Network Rail. The irregular passage of trains has meant that older infrastructure has lasted longer than in other corners of the UK rail network, but track renewal still takes place continually to bring the railway up to the required standards.

The view from a driver's perspective of the section of line above Loch Long where the railway crosses the Highland Boundary Fault. The sensors visible beneath the track are used to monitor any earth tremors, while the fence can detect any rockfalls. Note also the check rail, which provides stability on the steep hillside. (Author, cab ride with permission of ScotRail)

One recognisable trait of the Oban, Fort William and Mallaig routes these days is the 'clickety-clack' rhythm of trains moving across lengths of jointed track. Large sections of this are still in abundance, though they are gradually disappearing and being replaced by the noise-free, continuously-welded rail seen on most UK lines. Traditional bullhead rail is also found on many parts and being replaced as it becomes life-expired. Track sleepers are a mix of wooden, concrete and steel varieties. In addition, check rails are provided at many parts along all three routes to provide stability on sharp curves or sections where the railway climbs along high mountain ledges.

Since the introduction of the relatively lightweight Sprinters, there have been different speed restrictions in force to cater for them. They have a maximum speed of 55mph from Crianlarich–Oban, while for loco-hauled trains it is just 50mph.

On the Mallaig Extension east of Glenfinnan, it is 40mph for loco-haulage and 55mph for Sprinters. West of Glenfinnan it is 30mph for loco-haulage and up to 40mph for Sprinters.

On the Craigendoran–Fort William section, things are more complicated. In addition to the many restrictions over certain bridges and viaducts (especially for Class 66s and 67s), the relative line speed for Sprinters is 60mph, though there are a couple of short 70mph sections. Loco-haulage faces a restriction of 40mph from Craigendoran to Milepost 46 near Bridge of Orchy, thereafter mostly 50mph, though the limit is 60mph between Spean Bridge and Fort William Junction. There are even more restrictions for freights, which have a maximum limit of either 30 or 40mph throughout.

The early part of 2013 saw a major programme of engineering work in the West Highlands. A large amount of track renewal took place over several weeks

During an engineers' possession just south of Crianlarich on 3 March 2013, a mechanical road-rail vehicle collects old sections of wooden-sleepered bullhead rail for disposal. The newly-laid continuously welded track can be seen in the background. (Author)

in February and March on the southern part of the Glasgow–Fort William line, while there was also some re-ballasting on the Oban and Mallaig routes.

Ballast-dropping trains are the most frequent type of engineers' workings to be seen in the area. In recent times, they have appeared over the Oban and Mallaig routes around once a year (Class 37-hauled), using Network Rail JJA 'Autoballaster' wagons, which were first debuted in the West Highlands during 2001. These run in semi-permanent rakes of five, sometimes doubled up to form a ten-wagon load. Engineers' possessions are not required for the ballast drops, which normally take place during daytime hours between scheduled passenger trains.

Luckily most of the wayside stations on the West Highland lines have retained their sidings through the years and most are still in use by engineers' vehicles, with access controlled by ground frames. The main base for the permanent way department is the Up sidings at Crianlarich, where a small depot has been established for many years around the former North British Railway single-road locomotive shed, still standing to this day. Its use for housing track maintenance vehicles has allowed it to survive, unlike its former neighbouring turntable, which was removed at the end of the steam era.

A plethora of different track maintenance vehicles can be seen over the West Highland lines nowadays. Formerly all were owned by BR and painted yellow to denote their use for civil engineers' duties. Plasser & Theurer tampers, used to 'tamp' ballast into place around the track, have always been a regular sight up and down the line. A similar, more modern vehicle used by Network Rail today is the Multi-Purpose Vehicle (MPV), which is used for weedkilling or sandite duties. A variety of more lightweight vehicles have also been developed, many of which are 'road-railers': road vehicles which also have flanged wheels which can be lowered to allow them to travel along the railway line.

Land Rovers and lorries converted for use as 'road-railers' are regularly used by Network Rail maintenance teams for inspecting the track. The beauty of using these vehicles is that they can be driven along main roads to reach certain points of the line quicker and then placed on to the track by fitting their rail wheels into place. They are stopped on the middle of the single track sections (easily possible in the long gaps between trains) so that staff can inspect the four-foot for any breakages, loose or missing rail clips, or anything unusual. Carcasses of dead sheep and deer on the line also have to be removed and reported. All of the Land Rovers must be fitted with portable RETB equipment so that they can be used for the aforementioned tasks.

However, there were never such luxuries as road-rail Land Rovers, or even mobile phones, during the 1970s and 1980s, when track inspections required more time out walking on foot. One regular practice was for the daily Crianlarich–Corpach loaded timber train to drop off a track inspector at

Rannoch, who would then walk the entire 16-mile stretch of line across the moor back to Bridge of Orchy!

Other

Travellers and line-side photographers will notice there are a surprisingly large amount of platelayers' huts and line-side cottages still in existence today along all three routes in the West Highlands, though most have inevitably become derelict. A few of the cottages were refurbished and made available as holiday homes in recent years, such as one at Kinloid, near Arisaig. Snow fences on Rannoch Moor – erected in the early days of the railway to protect it during the worst of winters – have also stood the test of time.

All level crossings are now controlled automatically, with traditional gates being replaced by warning lights – either with or without modern barriers. The one at

Morar station and level crossing. (Author)

Corpach station was converted to an open type but was eventually given barriers in February 2013, after a number of motorists were involved in near misses with trains. These are of a new 'stubby' half-barrier type, installed as part of a £4 million campaign to improve safety at level crossings across the UK.

Morar could potentially get the same treatment – it has had an open, automatic crossing since its gates were removed in May 1985. Prior to this, even into the Class 37 era, approaching trains in either direction had to stop so that a train-crew member (either the guard or secondman) could open the gates and then close them again once the train had passed. Nowadays, the warning lights and siren of the crossing are activated by approaching northbound trains through track circuiting. In the opposite direction, all trains must stop at the station, where the driver (or fireman) has to activate the lights by pressing a plunger at the platform end. A white trackside light will come on to tell the train to proceed.

The Mallaig Extension has three other main level crossings: one next to Banavie station and two at Annat (next to the site of Corpach paper mill). All are controlled from Banavie signalling centre, with the latter two operated using CCTV. There are also a large number of user-worked accommodation or occupation crossings along all three West Highland routes, many of which are regularly used by local farmers. Those wishing to cross with a vehicle must first telephone Banavie signalling centre for permission. The swing bridge over the Caledonian Canal at Banavie is also controlled by the signalling centre, with a 5mph speed restriction in force over the structure. Further north, Glenfinnan Viaduct has a restriction of 25mph.

Near Milepost 16 on the line between Glen Douglas and Arrochar, there is special track equipment in place where the railway crosses the Highland Boundary Fault high above Loch Long. There is a 25mph speed limit and sensors placed under the rails here to detect any earth tremors and subsequent track movements, while a trackside fence detects any rockfalls, similar to that in the Pass of Brander. In addition, the former signal box at Glen Douglas had a warning system in place whereby any tremors in the mountain would cause a red light to flash. This was specifically a safety measure for the signalman and his family, who lived in the house next to the box, though the light is never thought to have been activated throughout its existence.

10

Signalling

Semaphore Signalling/Electric Token Block

In common with most other single-track routes in Scotland, the West Highlands used the traditional electric token block system for many years, controlled by signal boxes and semaphore signals at stations and crossing loops. This system was in use from the first days of the railway right up until 1988, when RETB was fully implemented. Before entering any single-track section, each train driver would have to be presented with the 'token', which gave him permission to enter the line ahead (thus not allowing more than one train to be in the section at any given time). Each token took the form of a brass disc (tablet) or key, held in a leather pouch with a large metal hoop to allow it to be handed over to the secondman of each passing train without them having to stop.

Inside each signal box, at the start/end of a single-track block section, the token was kept inside a special instrument, being electrically activated (through telegraph wires) once a bell code was sent from the next box down the line to notify of an approaching train. The signalman would then exchange tokens with the secondman, usually on the station platform. This was normally a double exchange – the signalman would hand over the pouch for the next section while taking the one from the preceding section. For example, at Spean Bridge a westbound train would surrender the Tulloch–Spean Bridge token and obtain the Spean Bridge–Fort William one.

If trains were not stopping, then they would have to pass through at slow speed to allow a token handover to take place. In practice, it was typically done at a higher speed than what was in the rulebook, especially with a heavy train on a gradient where too much of a drop in speed would cause the locomotive(s) to stall. The eastbound ascent through Dalmally was one such place.

Despite the Oban line being LMS territory and Glasgow–Fort William–Mallaig being LNER, the fundamentals of signalling were much the same. Lattice-post semaphores ruled over both; mostly ex-Caledonian Railway designs on the

Formerly possessing a crossing loop, which allowed more flexibility between Fort William and Mallaig, Lochailort is now a single-platform request stop. First ScotRail 'Barbie'-liveried 156458/476 trundle through on 24 June 2013 with the 0903 Glasgow–Mallaig. Note how, unusually, the white part of the leading unit's body-side stripe does not continue on to the cab front at one side. (Author)

former and North British versions on the latter. Lower quadrant semaphore arms were prevalent over both too, though most had been replaced by upper quadrant arms by the time diesel power took over. Those that had not soon would be. Most of the lattice posts survived in place, though a few were replaced by more modern BR tubular post designs.

Tokenless block was a method of working the single line using just signals and no token, and this was established between Crianlarich and Rannoch in 1967. Bi-directional running was authorised through the Down loop at Tyndrum Upper and the Up at Bridge of Orchy. This allowed the signal boxes here to 'switch out' when not required – usually at weekends. The year 1985 saw the use of tokens come back into play but not for long, with replacement by RETB just around the corner.

Of the semaphores in place along all three routes, some were mounted on very tall posts, which gave drivers better visibility. Crianlarich still had a distinctive lattice-post bracket signal controlling the junction to Oban until 1985, while Oban itself had a small semaphore gantry on the approach to its platforms. There were formerly two boxes here – one at the station (Oban station box) and one at the junction of the old goods yard and locomotive depot (Oban Goods Junction box) a quarter mile south of this. In May 1969, Oban Goods Junction box closed and the goods yard and station sidings were altered to a more simplified arrangement.

In December 1982, Oban station signal box also closed, as the station was reduced from four to two platforms. All semaphore signals were removed, with 'no signalman' key token working brought in between Oban and Taynuilt. Further north on the Extension line, the semaphore signals were gone at Mallaig too. The signal box here lost its status as a block post in March 1982, though it remained in place to control the station points. Following this, 'one-train working' became the norm between Arisaig and Mallaig.

Further rationalisation saw Arisaig signal box close in December 1983, with the semaphores removed and the crossing loop switched out of use, seemingly no longer required. As a result, one-train working was extended to the entire Glenfinnan–Mallaig section. However, automatic, spring-loaded points were put in place early the following year and the loop was brought back into use once the Fort William–Mallaig steam operation kicked off.

As mentioned earlier, semaphore signals were removed from most stations on the West Highland lines in 1985 and 1986, though the electric token system itself continued in use until full RETB control came into place in 1987 and 1988. This saw signal boxes stay open to allow token exchanges. Long section tokens also became available, such as those used between Spean Bridge and Rannoch. Prior to this, in 1985, all distant signals were removed, to be replaced by reflectorised distant boards to give a permanent 'caution' aspect on the approach to stations.

Fort William Junction signal box is still in use at the time of writing, with some fine lattice-post semaphores under its control. However, the box may not survive in the long term, now that Network Rail has announced plans to replace all mechanical signal boxes over the next thirty years. Annat signal box managed to survive until quite recently – being decommissioned and demolished in October 2011, when control of its level crossings was transferred to Banavie.

Radio Electronic Token Block (RETB)

All three of the West Highland routes have been under RETB control since 28 May 1988, when the Crianlarich–Fort William Junction section was added to become the final piece of the jigsaw. The fundamentals of this system are similar to the traditional electric token procedures, with trains still required to obtain the relevant token before heading into a single line section. Essentially the only difference is that the token is a virtual one, obtained through radio contact between the train driver and signaller, based in the Banavie control centre.

Most token exchange points on the lines are at crossing loops. When a train arrives at a token exchange point, the driver must pull up behind the 'STOP' board placed at the end of the loop. The driver will then make radio contact with the signaller, using their in-cab equipment, to report their position and press the 'SEND' button on their cab display unit (CDU) to return the token for the previous section.

The driver will then request the token for the next section of line ahead. If it is permitted, the driver will press the 'RECEIVE' button and the new token should be displayed in writing on the CDU. The LCD screen will display for instance 'Garelochhead/Arrochar', the same way as the traditional brass token would have it engraved. Once the driver has confirmed that the correct token is on display, they should be allowed to proceed with their journey towards the next token exchange point.

RETB token exchanges can only be made when a train is stopped. This means that whatever the type of train or locomotive, even if it is a freight or track maintenance vehicle, they must normally stop at nearly all of the token exchange points on their journey. All stations with crossing loops are token exchange points, though long section tokens can be permitted to bypass certain ones, which are described as 'intermediate' token exchange points. Ardlui and Corrour are often bypassed, while the non-station loop at Glen Douglas is also not a scheduled stop unless there is a crossing due to take place.

There are also token exchange points at a few stations without crossing loops – for instance Loch Eil Outward Bound, Connel Ferry and Tyndrum Lower, where drivers are still sometimes required to stop. This allows the lengthy single track

At the controls of Class 156 No 156457, ScotRail driver John Hanlon makes radio contact with the signaller during a stop at Garelochhead. The radio and cab display unit (CDU) can be clearly seen. (Author, taken during a cab ride with permission of ScotRail)

section in each case to be split into two shorter sections – this has been effective since the beginning of RETB operations. For RETB to work, it also requires several radio frequency changes en route and there are line-side signs informing drivers when to do this.

After joining the West Highland main line at Craigendoran, northbound trains enter the RETB signalling area for the first time just south of Helensburgh Upper station, leaving the jurisdiction of Yoker signalling centre (which controls the electrified main line to the south). This is known as the 'handshake', with a line-side board advising drivers accordingly. The opposite happens at the same point for southbound trains, with a colour light signal at the south end of Helensburgh Upper heralding the start of conventional signalling. Trains will therefore stop at Helensburgh Upper either to obtain their first RETB token if they are heading north, or to give up their last one if they are heading south. Locomotives without RETB equipment cannot operate any further north of the station.

The RETB-signalled area is only disrupted once north of here, at Fort William, where Fort William Junction signal box controls a short section around the junction of the Glasgow/Mallaig lines. The whole area from Tom-na-Faire depot to the aluminium plant siding on the Glasgow line, including the line into the town station, is controlled by semaphores and colour lights – anything to the north/east of here is RETB territory. However, operation involves a crossover of the two types of signalling, as trains arriving/departing Fort William station will still need to send/receive radio tokens here, even though colour light signals are in operation.

One of the key changes that came as a result of RETB was the conversion of most station loop points to spring-loaded operation. Not requiring a signalman or even so much as the push of a button, the points at each end of the loop are automatically set to bring an incoming train into the correct side (normally the left-hand side). Upon leaving the loop and approaching the set of points at the other end, the train's wheels will push the switch blades across in the required direction to let it out. They will then automatically return to place once the train has passed over them, with no operating personnel required. It also allows trains to pass one another at stations with no difficulty – often arriving and departing simultaneously.

The new signalling system also saw many station crossing loops altered for right-hand running, instead of the normal left (Up platforms became Down and vice versa). Those affected were Garelochhead, Ardlui, Bridge of Orchy, Rannoch, Spean Bridge and Taynuilt. It was done to allow easier access to the sidings, which all became operated by ground frames. Gorton and Corrour crossing loops became ground-frame-operated too, as their loops were generally just used by permanent way crews.

Another necessary piece of equipment is points set indicators, which look similar to colour light signals and are placed one at each end of a loop to face trains arriving at the station. When a train approaches, the indicator must display a yellow light to confirm that the loop points are correctly set. If they are not, the indicator will display a red light and the driver must make an emergency stop, then use the provided point clamp to set the road ahead. The red light is a recent addition – previously the indicator would just be unlit in this situation.

At Crianlarich, the junction points are set by drivers using a plunger at the end of the platform. There is a special points set indicator with a digital display that

An example of one of the 'STOP' boards which are nowadays placed at the start of each block section, including most stations, to tell the driver to obtain the relevant electronic token. Autumn 2003 saw Train Protection & Warning System (TPWS) also installed on the West Highland lines. The continuous blue light on each of the 'STOP' boards indicates that TPWS is working correctly, though it will flash when a token is issued and the system is deactivated temporarily. (Author)

will light up 'M' (main line) to show that the points are set towards Fort William, and 'B' (branch) if set towards Oban. The joining and splitting of passenger trains (ever since the introduction of Sprinters) has always added an extra few minutes at best to station stops here. When the separate Oban/Fort William portions are joined, the late running of one or both of them has been known to result in longer delays on occasions.

On most services, the Oban portion is scheduled to get the road into Crianlarich station first when the trains are joined. There are intermediate 'STOP' boards at the former site of Crianlarich Lower Junction and at the northern end of Strath Fillan Viaduct, where at least one of the joining portions must wait until they have authority from Banavie to proceed into the station. Most trains other than Sprinters can usually bypass these boards.

Also placed along the line are 'loop clear' marker boards, which indicate to the driver that their train is clear of the crossing loop at each location. Once passed, the driver must make radio contact with Banavie to confirm this.

Banavie signalling centre, today operated by Network Rail, has two workstations controlling the West Highland lines. The 'south' desk controls operations on the Helensburgh–Upper Tyndrum and Crianlarich–Oban sections, while the 'north' desk controls Upper Tyndrum–Mallaig. Each is operated by a single member of staff. The railway is often open through the night, typically for use by engineers' vehicles, so the signalling centre will be staffed during these hours too.

The introduction of RETB saw the single-manning of locomotive crews take place, with a secondman no longer being required. The system brings great communication benefits to drivers, in that it can be used for the signaller to warn of anything unusual, such as weather-related problems or permanent way gangs to look out for. The equipment can occasionally prove faulty, with poor radio reception being a typical problem, especially in bad weather, though reception has improved in recent years.

The RETB system in use on the West Highland lines is currently in the process of being upgraded, due to a change in radio frequencies in December 2015, when the work is scheduled for completion. While some radio equipment will be replaced, the basic operation will remain the same.

'Anderson's Piano'

The unique stone signals in the Pass of Brander, described earlier in the book, have remarkably stood the test of time on the railway for over 130 years. And they have remained relatively unaltered throughout. There are seventeen in total – covering a length of track of just over 4 miles – fifteen of which have two

Signal No 5 in the 'Anderson's Piano' section on the Oban line. Note that the westbound arm is at danger on this occasion. There has been no rockfall, however; it appears that something else, perhaps an animal, has triggered the signal and drivers have been made aware, so they are allowed to proceed at normal speed until the signal is reset. (Author)

West Highland Railway architecture at Bridge of Orchy. Whilst the main building is restored to its original condition and used as a bunkhouse, the signal box in the foreground is boarded up. (Author)

semaphore arms (one for each direction). The other two, at the respective far ends of the section, have single arms. All have lattice posts and upper quadrant arms, though they were originally lower quadrant before replacement in the 1960s.

All the signal arms are set in the 'clear' position under normal circumstances. The wire screen used to detect rockfalls runs alongside the trackbed through the section. If a single wire breaks, it causes the two nearest signals to drop to 'danger'. When a train driver notices a signal at danger he will normally proceed through the section at a very low speed. This is because from time to time the wires can be tripped by sources other than rockfalls, such as animals, when there are no obstructions on the line.

11

The Lines Today

While it was largely freight traffic that kept the West Highland lines open following Beeching, it is the thriving passenger levels that are key to their survival today. If anything, the recent recession has benefited the railway, with more tourists seemingly shunning expensive foreign destinations and visiting the Highlands instead. The revamped ScotRail timetable and longer train lengths are evidence of this – particularly at the height of the summer season when packed carriages are commonplace to Oban, Fort William and Mallaig. Even during the winter when loadings are far lighter, there are still decent amounts of foreign tourists and visiting coach parties on board at times. Though it is not just tourism – ScotRail's trains are also well used by local travellers at all times of the year.

The retention of Caledonian MacBrayne's ferry connections at Oban and Mallaig is vital for the future of the lines, as they provide for a large proportion of the traffic. At Oban, the forthcoming six-train-per-day service will allow even better transport integration of this nature, though there is a certain amount of public feeling that an improvement in rolling stock is required to build on these recent successes. The Friends of the West Highland Lines continue to campaign for new trains to really do the railway justice, but as yet there appears to be no short-term replacement for the Class 156 Sprinters. Locomotive-haulage is another interesting subject and indeed it has been re-established successfully along many rural lines following privatisation. But along with high costs and difficulties in sourcing the rolling stock, the lack of platform capacity at Glasgow Queen Street and Edinburgh Waverley would likely prevent their return to the West Highlands.

Late 2011 saw the 'Caledonian Sleeper' under major threat for the second time, with Transport Scotland publishing a consultation to review the future of Scotland's railway services. With the current ScotRail franchise originally due to finish in April 2014 and funding arrangements being revised, one option being considered was to reduce its sphere of operations.

Thankfully, helped by more local and political opposition, the sleeper was retained once again. Not only that, the government has pledged to invest

£50 million to upgrade or replace the existing rolling stock in the next few years. Originally, the figure given was £100 million, though half of this will now go towards other line improvements in the country. April 2015 will see a new Train Operating Company take charge of the sleeper service, which is being franchised separately. The main ScotRail franchise is expected to change hands at the same time.

The 'Jacobite' operation in particular is flying high at the present moment. Both morning and afternoon trains regularly run fully booked, with limited numbers of 'on-the-day' tickets usually snapped up very quickly after advance bookings have been made. And what a difference this makes to the economy of Mallaig in particular, where hundreds of tourists – many visiting from all over the world – descend upon the coastal town every day during the train's two-hour layover.

Sprinter No 156485 pauses at Banavie with the 1221 Glasgow–Mallaig on 26 June 2013, passing the signalling centre which controls the entire West Highland network. Banavie formerly had its own station building, as well as a timber-built signal box which was knocked down after RETB signalling came into force. (Author)

After leaving Banvie station, the 1221 Glasgow–Mallaig train slowly negotiates the swing bridge over the Caledonian Canal. The structure clearly needs a lick of paint! (Author)

The connection between the morning steam train and the sleeper at Fort William is also vital, something which would have been lost if the latter had been axed. Not only does the sleeper provide the only direct link between Lochaber and London, it is also a useful local service. Following daytime seated accommodation being reintroduced on the train in the late 1990s, it can now be used by ordinary passengers from stations north of Edinburgh. This option is especially popular with hillwalkers and climbers.

Looking back to the era of the 'Beeching Cuts', the West Highland lines are clearly now in a stronger position than before. Rewind fifty years and it would be hard to imagine the railway being the cult phenomenon that it is today, during a time when rural lines were looked at by the government as loss-makers and nothing else. Railway enthusiasts and the local community aside, there was little to support it, whereas today there are a number of groups – including the Friends of the West Highland Lines, HITRANS and ScotRail themselves – who promote the railway to encourage not just patronage, but recognition. Previously the lines were known to people up and down the UK and perceived to be some of the most scenic in the country. Now they are known all over the globe, as the best in the *world*.

Even the image of Glenfinnan Viaduct seen on Bank of Scotland ten pound notes today is testament to the high regard in which the West Highland lines are held. Continued work from the many hard-working volunteers and support groups will ensure that this continues to be the case. Another positive sign in this respect is that community rail partnerships are beginning to be established in Scotland following their success south of the border.

The remains of old bridges and platforms still stand today on the trackbeds of those lines lost to Beeching – namely the branches to Ballachulish and Killin, plus the former main line to Oban via Callander. One can only imagine what huge potential these wonderfully scenic lines would have for tourists today, even if one had managed to survive in some form as a preserved railway. At least some strides have been made in this way at Invergarry on the former Fort Augustus branch line, where volunteers are in the process of rebuilding the old station and forming a museum. It is certainly hard to imagine any of these lost lines being closed in today's era.

The post-Beeching era has certainly been an interesting time for the West Highland lines and at the end of the day, it is important to return to the fact that so little has changed aesthetically. A journey along the railway still reveals the same magnificent views and feats of engineering which captured travellers' imaginations fifty years ago – and now more people are aware of it. But as well

'Black Five' No 44871 leaves a plume of smoke as it climbs the hill west of Lochailort towards the distant church at Polnish, with the afternoon 'Jacobite' to Mallaig on 24 June 2013. (Author)

as appreciating the grandeur of what remains, it is also interesting to look at it the opposite way round, to examine what is new to the West Highland lines. They have been adapted to suit modern infrastructure such as radio signalling and state-of-the-art foreign-built locomotive types, such as the Class 67s. It is certainly intriguing to watch this smoothly-operated twenty-first-century West Highland railway in action and see how it compares to that of fifty years before.

Gradient Profiles

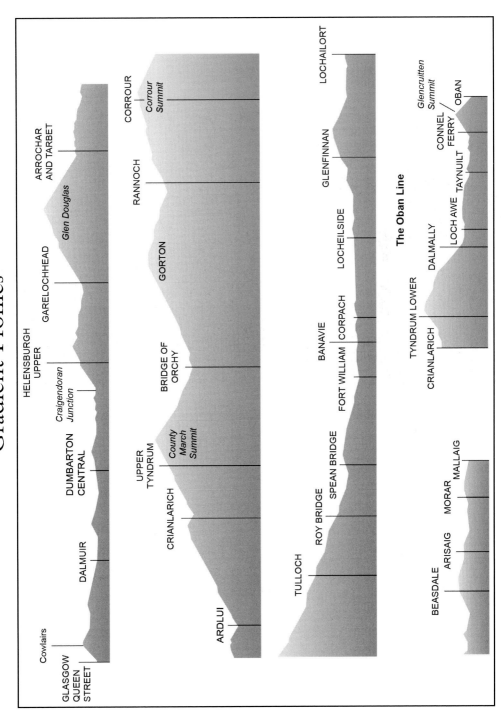

The Oban Line

Bibliography

Books

Dow, G., *The Story of the West Highland: The 1940s LNER Guide to the Line*, reprinted Northern Books, Famedram Publishers Ltd (2001).

Dunn, P., *The Power of the 20s*, OPC Railprint (2007).

Fox, P., *British Railways Pocket Book No.3: DMUs & Light Rail Systems*, 1996 Edition, Platform 5 (1996).

Hodgins, D. & Sanders, K., *North West Scotland,* Past and Present Publishing (1998).

Holland, J., *Amazing and Extraordinary Railway Facts*, David & Charles (2007).

Hunt, J., *Working the Jacobite: From the Footplate on the Road to the Isles*, HPE Print (2008).

McGregor, J., *100 years of the West Highland Railway*, ScotRail (1994).

McGregor, J., *The West Highland Railway: Plans, Politics and People*, John Donald (2005).

Mullay, A.J., *Scottish Region: A History 1948–1973 (British Railways Region by Region)*, The History Press (2006).

Noble, T., *The West Highland Mallaig Extension in B.R. Days*, OPC Railprint (1989).

Noble, T., *Profile of the Class 26s and 27s*, OPC (1982).

Pearson, M., *Iron Roads to the Isles: A Travellers and Tourists Souvenir Guide to the West Highland lines*, Third Edition, Wayzgoose (2009).

Thomas, J., *The West Highland Railway,* Third Edition, David St. John Thomas (1984).

Various, *Scottish Scenic Routes*, Ian Allan (1985).

Webb, B., *Sulzer Diesel Locomotives of British Rail*, David & Charles (1978).

Websites

www.uksteam.info
www.railbrit.co.uk
www.derbysulzers.com
www.c37lg.co.uk
www.therailwaycentre.com
www.oban-line.info
www.railuk.info
www.raib.gov.uk
www.scot-rail.co.uk
www.visit-fortwilliam.co.uk
www.highland.gov.uk
www.hansard.millbanksystems.com

Magazines

The Railway Magazine
Rail
Model Rail
Traction
Entrain
Railways Illustrated
Steam Railway

Videos

Railscene – various, Railscene Ltd (1986–90).
Steam to Mallaig, Video 125 (1985).
The Ultimate Scenic Route: The West Highland Line, Video Highland (1988).
Year of the Oban line, Video Highland (1986).

Media

Lochaber News
The Herald
The Guardian
The Independent
BBC News

Index